ESSENTIAL PSYCHOLOGY

General Editor
Peter Herriot

F6

HOW DO WE CHOOSE?
A study in consumer behaviour

ESSENTIAL

PSYCHOLOGY

HOW DO WE CHOOSE?

A study in consumer behaviour

Mary Tuck

Methuen

For my mother

First published in 1976 by Methuen & Co Ltd
11 New Fetter Lane, London EC4P 4EE
© 1976 Mary Tuck
Printed in Great Britain by
Richard Clay (The Chaucer Press), Ltd
Bungay, Suffolk

ISBN (hardback) 0 416 81990 7
ISBN (paperback) 0 416 82330 0

We are grateful to Grant McIntyre of
Open Books Publishing Ltd for assistance
in the preparation of this series

Acknowledgements

Many of the ideas in this book have been discussed with friends and colleagues over the years. I am grateful to many, but must thank in particular Dr Elizabeth Nelson of Taylor-Nelson Associates, Dr Kerry Thomas of Imperial College and, most of all, my husband Robin Tuck. All three have discussed the ideas in this book many times. None of them would agree with everything I say. None of them have read the book in advance. But they have all influenced it, and I am grateful to them.

Contents

Editor's Introduction

Many of us feel that we are putty in the hands of the manipulators: advertisers, politicians, persuaders of all sorts. Mary Tuck shows clearly that the only satisfactory account of our actions as consumers is one of conscious choice. After demonstrating the unsatisfactory nature of many current approaches to consumer behaviour, Mary Tuck introduces the theory of Fishbein. He sees intentions to act as the products of our attitudes and beliefs, and his theory has applications extending far beyond consumer behaviour.

How Do We Choose? belongs to Unit F of Essential Psychology. What unifies the books in this unit is the concept of change, not only in people but also in psychology. Both the theory and the practice of the subject are changing fast. The assumptions underlying the different theoretical frameworks are being revealed and questioned. New basic assumptions are being advocated and consequently new frameworks constructed. One example is the theoretical framework of 'mental illness': the assumptions of normality and abnormality are being questioned, together with the notions of 'the cause', 'the cure', and 'the doctor-patient relationship'. As a result, different frameworks are developing, and different professional practices gradually being initiated. There are, though, various social and political structures which tend to inhibit the translation of changing theory into changing practice.

One interesting change is the current aversion to theoretical frameworks which liken human beings to something else. For example, among many psychologists the analogy of the human being as a computer which characterizes Unit A is in less favour than the concepts of development (Unit C) and the person (Unit D).

Essential Psychology as a whole is designed to reflect this changing structure and function of psychology. The authors are both academics and professionals, and their aim has been to introduce the most important concepts in their areas to beginning students. They have tried to do so clearly, but have not attempted to conceal the fact that concepts that now appear central to their work may soon be peripheral. In other words, they have presented psychology as a developing set of views of man, not as a body of received truth. Readers are not intended to study the whole series in order to 'master the basics'. Rather, since different people may wish to use different theoretical frameworks for their own purposes, the series has been designed so that each title stands on its own. But it is possible that if the reader has read no psychology before, he will enjoy individual books more if he has read the introductions (A1, B1 etc.) to the units to which they belong. Readers of the units concerned with applications of psychology (E, F) may benefit from reading all the introductions.

A word about references in the text to the work of other writers – e.g. 'Smith (1974)'. These occur where the author feels he must acknowledge an important concept or some crucial evidence by name. The book or article referred to will be listed in the References (which double as Name Index) at the back of the book. The reader is invited to consult these sources if he wishes to explore topics further.

We hope you enjoy psychology.

Peter Herriot

Introduction

Of course some people think we never choose. We are victims or creatures of our class, of our past learning, of our masters; poor conditioned creatures who creep through the world in a condition of semi-awareness, never discriminating for ourselves, always manipulated, unable to exercise anything so illusory as free will.

But our own experience of ourselves is other. We have the 'feeling' that it is up to us whether we decide to watch one programme or another on television, to go home from work by bus or tube, to buy one sort of toothpaste or another. In some confused way we are pretty certain that our own decisions, our own 'choices', have something to do with the actions we take. Though as these examples show, we are perfectly aware that our choices are limited. We cannot decide to watch a television programme that is not available, to go home by a Rolls-Royce and chauffeur if we can't afford it, and maybe we never buy our own toothpaste but leave it to wife or mother or someone else to buy it for us. But whatever the restriction on our choice, we do have a feeling that we have *some*. Our every action of every day is not predictable or conditioned. Every day indeed there is a weight of decisions to be made in little things that can even become wearisome. Shall I wait for the bus at this bus-stop, or will it be quicker to go for the tube? Would cabbage be a good thing to buy for dinner, or would the family rather have carrots? Should I let the children watch 'Match of the Day' or insist on the programme on the other side that I would rather have? Sometimes one gets the feeling that every minute, every hour is full of these small choices. And sometimes, if we are in philosophic mood, we may speculate as to why we make the choices we do. And speculate too, if the machinery by which we make these choices is the same or other as the machinery by which we make more far-reaching choices. Whom shall I marry, shall I marry at all, do I really want children, is it a good idea to join the Communist party, is it worth while going to work or school at all, or should I just give up and stay in bed?

So we ourselves are interested in 'how we choose', partly in order to understand ourselves, partly in order to convince ourselves that we are in any sense at all free agents. And we are not the only people interested in 'how we choose'. There are other people out there watching us. Television programmers who want to know how they can persuade us to watch their programme not the other, manufacturers who want us to buy the products of their factories, politicians who want us to vote for their party or work for their view of the future of the world, religious leaders who wish to convert us, market researchers whose trade is to discover what we choose and why we choose what we do, social psychologists who try to understand why we do what we do. They are all to some degree or other interested in understanding the grounds of our choice. And if you think about it, they all recognize to some extent that we *have* choice. If we all automatically did conditioned, predictable things, then no-one would be bothered trying to entice, persuade, convince, coerce others. In all the operations of day to day living, we go on 'as if' others had some independence of decision, some ways in which they themselves decide what they do. Even if the world is full of manipulators trying to persuade others, it is only because they believe these others have in usual circumstances a modicum of control over their own actions that the attempts at persuasion, conviction, coercion, brain-washing have any *raison d'être*.

This book is not a work of philosophy; I am not going to examine how reasonable it is to picture the human being as a person with 'choice' or examine in any very careful detail the meaning of the concept. What I am going to do is to look at the major theories extant in the world around us of how human beings do choose, to report on them, and to suggest another and different theory.

Who are the people who have developed the theories which are actually in use in our Western world? Foremost among them are the marketers. There is a whole area of academic marketing theory known as 'consumer behaviour theory'. Developed mainly in the United States, it is an attempt by marketers and economists to understand choice behaviour in the market place. It has grown up in Western capitalist societies, because the way capitalist societies are organized puts weight on the choice of individual consumers. In the centralized societies of the East, no-one is particularly interested in 'consumer behaviour' because consumers are expected to consume what is there. Centralized planners attempt to work out the means of transport, the kind of soap, the kind of housing, which it is best for that society to produce and consume, and then make it available. It is only Western society which is run on, at least theoretically, an 'open' principle. Many different things are available, whatever individual entrepreneurs can get out onto the market; and it is for individuals themselves to decide what they buy, and hence, in the long run, influence what is produced.

The difference described in the last paragraph is, of course, far too extremely stated. You may point out that in the capitalist West, large multi-national firms have the marketing process sewn up, so individual entre preneurs cannot get their products on the market for individuals to choose; or that in the centralized East, the State attempts more and more (as for instance in Hungary) to find means to let consumer choice influence centralized planning decisions as to what is made. But though you may quibble with the edges of my argument, a broad difference in theory and practice does exist. It is capitalist America which has hundreds of different kinds and brands of bread or soap available; Russia which has a few State-made kinds. So it is no accident that in capitalist America there has been much more impetus to study and understand the grounds of consumer choice.

In this book I want to examine and report to you on the major theories of consumer behaviour which have been developed in the schools of marketing. I will cover these in Chapter 1 of Part One of this book. But as well as the formal quasi-academic theories, there is a lot of work going on in the actual commercial world. Market researchers are employed in order to report on why people choose, large companies themselves attempt to operate on the mechanisms of choice; advertisers, television, media-owners all try to shift our choices, and they all operate according to some underlying theory. In Chapter 2 of Part One, I shall look at what I call 'implicit theories': the theories actually used by operators in the commercial world, which are not always the same as those taught in schools of marketing and courses on consumer behaviour. It is my hope that Chapters 1 and 2 of Part One will be of particular use to students of consumer behaviour in universities and technical colleges, both as a brief review of what they will be expected to know, and a reminder of what exists outside the academic world; and to practising advertisers, brand managers and marketing men, in introducing them to areas of theory they may not have studied, and helping them to think in a more careful way of the implicit theories underlying what they themselves do.

The consumerist view

But I do not want simply to speak to the marketers, whether in training in academic institutions, or in practice in the commercial world. The understanding of consumer behaviour has recently become a fashionable subject of study for others in our society. The huge new consumer movement, pioneered by people like Ralph Nader in the USA and Michael Young in Great Britain, has, I believe, suffered from lack of careful thought about the actual mechanisms of choice. Refuge has been taken in the rather paranoid theories of writers like Vance Packard, who see the consumer as a victim of totally manipulatory and evil forces. Or, because the consumerist movement – the *Which?* and the *Where?* magazines, the articles in *The Guardian* – has largely been staged by the middle classes for the middle classes, there has been altogether too unthinking an assumption that man is moved by argument alone; that rationality and logic, if they do genuinely underly all choice, *should* underly all choice. So the consumer movement has tended to engage in rather shrill denunciations of persuasions and messages which attempt to influence choice by non-logical means, and to see 'right' and 'virtue' only in the exer-

14

cises of 'pure logic'. The consumer movement is, to my mind, badly in need of a more sophisticated and intelligent understanding of the mechanisms of choice, and I hope this book will contribute towards that end.

The psychologist's view

But it is, after all, a text in a series called *Essential Psychology*, and it would not have found a place in this series if the Editor and myself did not believe that the discipline which has most to offer (and perhaps most to learn), in the study of consumer choice is the discipline of psychology. Group theory, conformity theory (see B2 of *Essential Psychology*), the theory of attitudes and behaviour (see B3), learning theory, the study of conditioning (see A3) . . . all these areas and many others are concerned with studying, explaining, experimenting, theorizing, on how, if at all, we decide to do what we do. Are we completely affected by our society, our group? Are we automatically programmed by our past learning experience? Do such things as attitudes exist and are they connected with behaviour?

It is entirely logical, that this book should come at the end of the *Essential Psychology* series: not because it covers the most important area of study, but because any theory of consumer choice developed today must utilize the background of knowledge built up by psychologists and must be in some sense dependent on the body of theory, experiment and analysis which has been briefly reviewed in all the other books in the series. I wish in this book, not only to review the theories which are currently popular as to 'how we choose', but to advance a new line of argument. Section I of the book will, as I have explained, cover reviews of existing theory. But in Part Two I intend to develop a more purely psychological account as to 'how we choose'. This section will, I hope, be of interest not only to those attracted to the particular applied area of consumer choice, but also to the theoretic psychologist, who may find that the discipline of trying to apply some concepts developed in pure psychology to practical problems of the modern world can illuminate and extend his purely psychological understanding.

Note on structure

To recapitulate on the structure of this text: in Part One I shall review existing theories of consumer choice. Chapter 1 will review academic theories of consumer behaviour. Chapters 2 and 3 will cover the theories in use in the marketing world, some of which are implicit rather than explicit theories.

In Part Two I shall look at the contribution made by psychologists to understanding consumer behaviour.

In Part Three I shall review the state of applied research at the present time, with particular reference to the United Kingdom.

And at the end of the book I shall try to draw some strands together and see what we have learned.

Part One
EXISTING THEORIES
OF CONSUMER
BEHAVIOUR

I
Academic theories of consumer behaviour

What exactly is 'consumer behaviour'? To many people the concept is familiar. Courses are taught in universities, there are journals of consumer behaviour, books on consumer behaviour. To others, the phrase may seem absurdly pretentious and ill-defined. Are we not all consumers in some sense, and is not all our behaviour therefore 'consumer behaviour'? What need for a special subject area?

To find out how the phrase is used in practice, it is simplest to look at one of the most widely used textbooks in the area, Engel, Kollat and Blackwell's *Consumer Behavior* (1967). Engel, Kollat and Blackwell define consumer behaviour as 'the acts of individuals directly involved in obtaining and using economic goods and services, including the decision processes that precede and determine these acts'. They write:

> The central purpose of this text, as well as of courses concerned with consumer behaviour, is to develop the ability to understand *why* individuals purchase what they do and how purchasing behaviour can be influenced by various members of a society.

So 'consumer behaviour' is really a field of study defined by its focus of interest, and that focus of interest is shopping, marketing, buying behaviour. The consumer behaviour theorist is interested in people's purchasing and consumption acts. Are there regular patterns in their behaviour? Can we understand it? Can we model it? Can we affect it? Two sorts of people have been interested in or have helped to construct these theories. Firstly there are the business academics, the people in schools of marketing or business management who see their task as reflecting on and coming to understand the confusions of the market-place. Secondly there are the practitioners; people involved in selling or marketing who wish to understand the activities they are trying to influence in order to influence them more effectively. Most of the formalized theories of consumer behaviour have come from the first group, but, as I shall hope to show, many different and influential theories have been elaborated by the practitioners, people involved in selling or marketing. Both practitioners and business school academics have constructed theories specially designed to deal with the consumer behaviour area as such. They have felt the right way to proceed has been to look at this particular section of human behaviour in detail and attempt to elaborate theories which would illuminate it.

It is not certain that this procedure is right, or that consumer behaviour will prove to be best understood through theories and models which have arisen from looking only at this particular section of human activity. The separation of the sector 'consumer behaviour' is somewhat artificial. The focus of interest may well be mistaken. Newton did not arrive at his theory of gravity through looking for theories on 'apple behaviour', through setting up courses on 'apple behaviour', journals in 'apple behaviour', stochastic theories of the likely number of apples to fall from a tree on any given day. He explained the behaviour of the apple through general theories drawn from a wider range of reference. It is possible that this too may be the best strategy for understanding the behaviour of consumers. But first we must take a look at such theories of specifically consumer behaviour which have been elaborated.

In a book of this length it will not be possible to review all the theories of consumer behaviour that have emerged over the last decades and have been taught in our business schools. However there are three main texts, three main theorists, whose work most students in business schools, or in departments of consumer behaviour are asked to cover. These I must report on. They are the work of Francesco M. Nicosia, who in 1966 made a serious and thorough attempt to reduce the unstructured muddle of then-current consumer behaviour theories to some set of equations that could be covered by computer simulation; the work of Engel, Kollat and Blackwell, who have produced one of the most widely read and studied books on consumer behaviour; and, lastly, the work of Howard and Sheth, whose book, *The Theory of Buyer Behavior*, published in 1969, remains one of the most up-to-date in the field.

Slightly aside from the work of the above theorists, have been the studies of observed empirical regularities in actual buying behaviour, of which the most sophisticated and intelligent have come from Andrew Ehrenberg of the London School of Business, which I shall discuss briefly at the end of this chapter.

Nicosia's theory

In a sense, Nicosia's work arose out of the computer revolution. As he put it:

> Digital computer simulation can handle systems of interactions where none of the many variables alone accounts for much of the variance or has an impact strong enough to determine the state of the system, but where all the variables simultaneously bear upon the state of the system. (p. 491)

In simple words, computers can handle complicated sums. They make technically possible the kind of calculations which depend on a lot of variables being considered together, and calculations made as to their effectiveness.

But what is necessary if any system is to be analysed by a computer is a 'model', a 'simulation system'. The interrelationship of variables has to be at least postulated, and reduced to a set of equations, before the numerical calculations can take over. The computer can do complex sums, but it can't tell you what sums to do. Your theory has to be reduced to a set of equations or sums before you can get the computer to work them out.

Nicosia attempted the Herculean task of reducing consumer behaviour theories and insights to a set of equations which the computer could model. As he wrote in the introduction to his work (p. xii) he wanted to 'take stock of various perspectives on the consumer in the field of marketing, economics and the

21

behavioural sciences' and to integrate these insights into a 'structural view that defines consumer behaviour as a decision process'. What he did essentially was to formularize other people's insights. He tells us the view he presents was constructed by 'selecting and then organising into structures, a great many of the variables and their functional relationships specified in the literature' (p. xiii). He tells us he wishes to describe the phenomena in terms of '(a) a list of variables that make up its content or morphology, and (b) a list of functional relations (or mechanisms or networks) through which the variables in (a) affect each other over time'.

Unfortunately, Nicosia's idea of a functional relationship is merely a statement that one variable, say y, is a function of another variable, say x. For instance, the state of my liver (y) is a function of what I have eaten (x). This is written in the form $y = f_y(x)$ or can be graphically represented by an arrow in a flow chart:

$$x \rightarrow y$$

Note that as written down above there is absolutely no specification of the *nature* of the relationship.

There is a further problem with how the variables that are linked by arrows or functions are selected. Nicosia's variables are largely a pot-pourri from introductory psychological texts. For instance, since dissonance research (see B3) has shown that sometimes behaviour (B) influences attitudes (A) we get two variables (B, A) and a functional relationship between them

or
$$\begin{array}{|l|} \hline A = fB \\ B \rightarrow A \\ \hline \end{array}$$

However, since it has also been argued that attitudes influence behaviour, a second functional relationship is necessary.

or
$$\begin{array}{|l|} \hline B = f_B A \\ A \rightarrow B \\ \hline \end{array}$$

Since it is assumed that a person's personality (P) can influence his reception of a message, we find that

$$R = f_R P$$

These kinds of statements are neither enlightening not necessarily consistent with psychological theory. Nicosia specifies very many of them. Ultimately they lead to an incredibly complex flow-chart containing a multitude of variables, most of which have not been operationalized (for example, transmission, exposure, motives, etc.) and whose precise relations to each other are unknown. Operationalized is an ugly word, but a useful one. It means that no measurement methods have been devised by which the variables concerned can be specified. Nicosia's flow-chart is too complex to reproduce satisfactorily on a page of this size, but Figure 1.1 represents a simplified version of this flow-chart, which is, perhaps, easier to look at and understand. Nicosia is postulating four sub-fields through which the consumer decision process moves. In Field One a

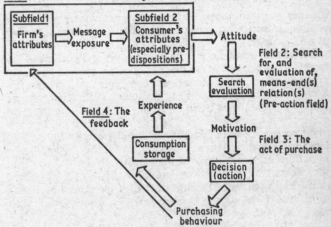

Fig. 1.1 *A summary flow-chart structure of consumer behaviour*
(Nicosia, 1968)

message emanates from a persuader (perhaps a commercial firm) and this is received and processed by a consumer and in some way issues as an attitude. This attitude is seen as an input to Field Two, where the consumer is postulated to carry out a search and evaluation process among rival brands and products. The output from Field Two is seen as a motivation to buy and serves as the input for Field Three. Field Three is the Act of Purchase; the transformation of motivation to buy into actual purchasing behaviour. This behaviour acts as an input for

Field Four, consumption of purchase, and/or storage. The output of Field Four feeds back into Field One to become part of the predispositions of the consumer which he or she will bring to bear on any succeeding message.

The function of Nicosia's simplified flow-chart is to suggest that the whole complicated 'how we choose' process can be boiled down to four equations based on four variables. The variables are:

B – the final act (buying brand X)
M – motivation
A – attitude
C – communication sent by a business firm

Neither motivation nor attitude are operationalized. C, the communication sent, could be operationalized as the number of dollars spent.

These four variables are the main inputs and outputs of the four fields described in the diagram. Nicosia goes on to reduce his basic scheme to just four linear equations based on assumptions about the relationship of attitudes, motivation, buying levels, and then uses these equations to derive some conclusions about varying the level of motivation, attitude or communications. If such conclusions could logically be derived from his equations they would be useful. We would know something more. We would mathematically have discovered the effect of varying say 'communication' (C in his equations) (measured perhaps in amount of dollars spent on a message), or of artificially varying behaviour itself, leaving other variables constant.

But the whole attempt founders for at least one simple reason. Nicosia has assumed, for simplicity, that there is a purely linear relationship between variables. But, where we have empirical knowledge, we know that the relationship is *not* linear. Psychologists have long known that behaviour is not a linear function of attitude (see B3). If motivation is at all like behaviour then it, too, will not be a linear function of attitude and Nicosia's equation 2 fails to hold. His other equations are open to similar criticism.

A system which will not hold
Nicosia made a brave attempt to bring order out of the chaos of eclectic consumer theory. He tried to reduce a set of insights

and assumptions to variables and equations which the computer could simulate, and from the mathematical statement of which further conclusions could be drawn. But his attempt was too ambitious and too premature. He tended to take broad psychological over-generalizations as given, so that he could enter everything into his flow chart. There is little or no concern with the operationalization of the variables listed in the flow chart. (Number of dollars spent is clearly an inadequate specification of the nature of a message.) There is little or no specification of the nature of the relationship between variables. What knowledge we have suggests that the simplifying assumption of a linear relationship is a falsification.

At least Nicosia, by his heroic attempt to reduce the eclectic mess that was consumer theory to four main equations, makes us aware of how much we do *not* know, of how many incompatible and unspecifiable entities, in unknown relationships with each other, are being pressed into service to explain consumer behaviour. Unfortunately recent research suggests most of his equations are either wrong or (worse still) untestable.

Its status as a 'theory'
Anyone who has an acquaintance with the history of science will see a strange similarity in Nicosia's 'theory' to the kind of theories or models of the behaviour of the stars and planets which were current before Newton's astronomy. Then the main requirement of a theory was that it should 'save the phenomena', that is, should be in accord with all the then-known descriptive facts. It was not held necessary that it should be testable. Nicosia's flow-chart is a pretty and elegant arrangement of one way by which consumer decision processes *might* happen; but the pathway modelled and suggested is only one among a wide variety of possibilities. He includes most of the 'phenomena' we are aware of in the consumer decision process; but gives us no reason to suppose that they really do interact in the way he proposes. He suggests for instance that Field Two (search and evaluation among rival products) succeeds Field One (reception of a message). But what about the consumer who for instance enters a tourist gift shop, never having before been aware of its contents? Messages and exposures about various products are going to be received at the same time as the evaluation process goes on. It is a small

25

point but could be repeated again and again. Acts of purchase (Field Three) frequently precede Field Two search and evaluation processes. The whole system is in terms of single brand choice and totally fails to grapple with the multi-purchase, multi-message, multi-choice situation of so much consumer behaviour. Again and again Nicosia's model can be seen to be just one among a possible multiplicity of models.

The central point is that Nicosia models for us one way in which consumer decision processes *might* happen, rather like the pre-Newtonian astronomers modelled for us ways in which the stars *might* behave. It would be mathematically and aesthetically pleasing if they so did. But there is no particular reason to think that they so do. What is worse, we can all, by introspection, arrive at direct experience of consumer decision processes which appear to contradict Nicosia's flow-chart.

Nicosia's theory must be accounted a brave failure. And though it continues to be discussed in departments of consumer behaviour and has some influence on computer simulations, it has never to my knowledge been seriously used in the making of marketing decisions. We turn now to an influential book, *Consumer Behavior* by Engel, Kollat and Blackwell (1968), which has become the backbone of consumer behaviour studies in many academic institutions in Europe and North America.

Engel, Kollat and Blackwell

Engel, Kollat and Blackwell, like Nicosia, produced a flow-chart. It is reproduced as Figure 1.2. Like Nicosia, they used the concepts of behavioural science in an attempt to model, in a way both detailed and capable of general applications, the processes which consumers must go through in decision. The chart at Figure 1.2 is once again only their *summary* chart, but in itself is of an awesome complexity. Once again it suffers from the defects of Nicosia's approach. The scheme drawn up may have a superficial plausibility, but there is no way suggested of testing it. We are still at the level of pre-scientific thinking. This is still a theory like those of the seventeenth-century cosmogonists designed simply to 'save the phenomena'.

Again, Engel, Kollat and Blackwell's model, like Nicosia's, suffers from the disadvantages of lack of specificity. Variables are named in a superficially plausible way, but not specified in any operational detail. For instance 'personality characteristics' (see D3) are included in a black box in the flow-chart (Fig. 1.2, top right-hand corner) but when we come to look at the chapter in which the authors spell out in detail the role of personality characteristics and personality measures in their model (Chapter 8), we learn:

> There has been no convincing demonstration of a consistent relationship between personality and persuasibility, social influence and product or brand choice . . . the yield of useful data when personality variables are used to predict buyer behaviour has been shown to be meager . . . the stage is now set for exciting new avenues of inquiry.

(Incidentally, the solecism of 'stage set for new avenues' is a typical example of Engel, Kollat and Blackwell's felicitous prose style; the book is no easy read.) What is this sentence really saying? It tells us that Engel, Kollat and Blackwell have no idea how personality characteristics should be measured to test or apply their model, they have no evidence that measuring personality characteristics helps to predict buyer behaviour in any way, but they feel 'personality characteristics' ought to be present in their model somewhere lest someone accuses them of lack of completeness. This approach is typical of the whole book. Again and again one turns to specific chapters to find how the authors suggest operationalizing various parts of their *a priori* model, and one finds no answer.

Howard and Sheth

A yet more ambitious theory of consumer behaviour, the theory of Howard and Sheth, was published in the year following Engel, Kollat and Blackwell's work (*The Theory of Buyer Behavior*, 1969). To my mind it suffers from the same defects as the work of their predecessors; it is, strictly speaking, pre-scientific. The theory produced is untestable and non-specific and fails to meet the criteria of a good science. However, since the authors themselves devote Chapters 1 and 10 of their book to arguing that their theory does fulfil the requirements of

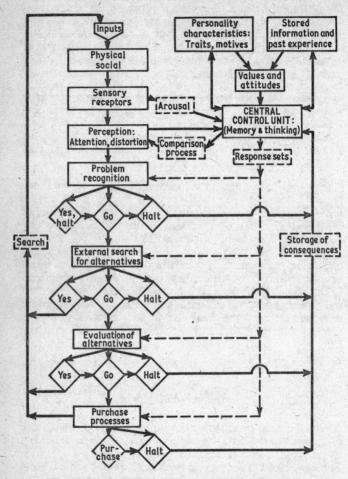

Fig. 1.2 *From Engel, Kollat and Blackwell, 1970*

scientific theorizing, some attention should be given to their arguments.

Before doing so, it will perhaps be best to spell out a little more fully what I mean by a good theory (see A1 and A8). There is nothing original or extraordinary about my criteria. In Great Britain, the work of Karl Popper has convinced a generation of their applicability; and Popper's ideas have been widely popularized and diffused by Peter Medawar (Popper, 1972; Medawar, 1967). In North America the work of Campbell has familiarized social scientists with a similar 'hypothetico-deductive' approach. Popper has argued that all universal laws or theories are in the nature of guesses or hypotheses. The theories of Newton were, until Einstein, the best guesses we had as to the problem of gravity. There never was a theory as well-established as Newton's, yet his theory has come, at the very least, under question as the result of Einstein's. As Popper puts it; 'whatever one may think about the status of Einstein's theory, it certainly taught us to look at Newton's as mere hypothesis or conjecture'. How then can one judge between 'good' theories and 'bad' theories, since all theories have the status of conjecture? Popper's answer is that we can judge by their falsifiability. It is of the nature of logic that it can never prove the absolute truth of a generalization or hypothesis. Though we may never yet have observed a golden swan, it is impossible to prove the truth of the statement 'Golden swans do not exist', because we do not know but that someday, somewhere, someone may observe one. We can however say that the statement 'Golden swans do not exist' is a meaningful statement, because it could be disproved in a quite specific way (by even a single observation of a golden swan) and because it fits the observable facts (that a golden swan has not yet been sighted). Thus, Popper has taught us, a 'good' theory is one that fits the observable facts, and is conceptually capable of disproof. Popper also suggested a further criterion of a good theory; its level of information content. It is possible to devise purely *ad hoc* theories which explain a very small set of events. These theories are not as powerful, as 'good', as those which can explain a larger set of events.

Now Howard and Sheth present formally in Chapters 1 and 10 their criteria for good theories. They list four: a good theory should fulfil a descriptive function, a delimiting function, an integrative function and a generative function.

The insistence on a 'descriptive function' for an hypothesis is an odd one. They expand by writing, 'If one has a pretzel, one must have a pretzel-shaped hypothesis to explain it.' This remark seems to me meaningless. If they mean that a theory must 'save the phenomena', to use the old terms, i.e. that it must be in accord with observed facts, then one must agree with them. But something more seems to be intended. They write, 'The theory must succeed in describing the phenomenon of buying behaviour.' One can only disagree with some puzzlement. A theory of buying behaviour is not the same thing as a description of buying behaviour.

It is easier to agree with their 'delimiting function'. By this they mean that a theory must delimit the meaning of the terms and variables it uses. 'The hypothesised relations must be able to be tested by comparing them with the corresponding relations among empirical facts.' Here indeed we gratefully and hopefully agree. A failure to delimit variables is precisely the fault on which the theories of Nicosia and Engel, Kollat and Blackwell founder.

Their third requirement for a theory is that it should be 'integrative'. If by this they meant that it should have a wide range of application, a high information content, then we would agree with them. But the concept appears more slippery. They want their theory to bring together diverse types of explanation. This is getting too close to eclecticism. Genuine integration is a quality highly to be valued, if it means a wider range of phenomena are explained. However a false integration, which means only the presentation within one theory of a wide range of contradictory concepts, is not to be so valued.

However it is the 'generative' function of a theory that they find most important, and it is here that the inadequacy of their grasp of what constitutes scientific thinking shows through most clearly. They write: 'To achieve a greater generative effect, we have tended to be somewhat loose and vague at times . . . We believe that our approach is more productive of fruitful hunches, ideas and new hypotheses. It leaves one free for imaginative theorising.' In other words they think a theory is a good theory if it raises a lot of imaginative ideas. Nowhere do they show any understanding of the need for a theory to be falsifiable, to be testable. If their theory fits the observed phenomena, and suggests bright new ideas they will be happy. All they are looking for is a 'plausible' picture. Indeed, they

conclude (p. 399): 'To summarise, all of the specific propositions generated from the theory predict the kind of buying
behaviour that we seem to observe. It is a plausible picture.
History will tell us whether it is an adequately true one for
now.' Burnet could have concluded his seventeenth-century
disquisition of the state of the world before the Flood in the
same way. Howard and Sheth are open to the same exasperated
comment which Peter Medawar made on Burnet's work: 'They
do not seem to realize that their hypothesis is but one among a
virtual infinity of hypotheses and that they are under a moral
obligation to find out if theirs is preferable to any other.'
Indeed they do not. 'Plausibility' and 'generative power',
'integration' and 'descriptive power' are what Howard and
Sheth are looking for. This is not science.

The actual model

Despite their philosophic discussion, which raised hopes that
they might understand the vacuity of so much preceding work,
Howard and Sheth's actual theory is very like those that preceded it. At Figure 1.3, we reproduce their main diagram. It
will be seen that it covers much the same range of variables
which were discussed by Nicosia and Engel, Kollat and Blackwell, but arranged in yet another arbitrary and untestable
pattern.

Howard and Sheth might retort to this criticism that their
model is testable by virtue of their principle of delimitations.
In their theoretic chapters they discuss the question of verifi-
ability and state that all intervening variables must be operationalized. Yet if one looks in their text for the operational
meaning of such variables as 'perceptual bias', for instance, one
looks in vain. Again and again the authors fail to suggest how
constructs defined in purely verbal terms could in fact be
measured. Their theory remains, therefore, without meaningful content and untestable.

Readers may like to be assured that I am not alone in viewing
most of the work of this particular school of North American
theorists of consumer behaviour as of little value. Professor
Ehrenberg of London School of Business, in a discussion of
the work of Howard and Sheth, points out that the only
conclusions of an attempt to test it made by Farley and Ring
in 1970 was that 'the test put extreme pressure on the data'
(not, as Ehrenberg points out, on the model!) and that 'con-

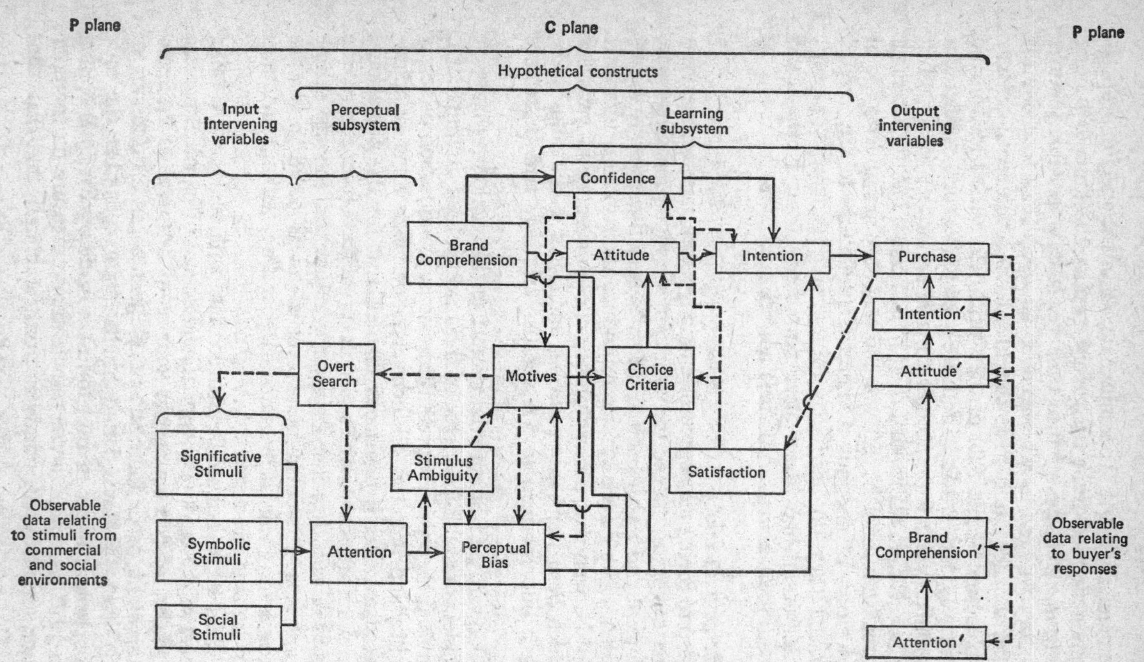

Fig. 1.3 *From Howard and Sheth, 1969*

P plane

Observable data relating to buyer's responses

C plane

Hypothetical constructs

Output intervening variables

Learning subsystem

Perceptual subsystem

Input Intervening variables

Purchase — 'Intention' — 'Attitude' — Brand Comprehension' — Attention'

Intention — Confidence — Attitude — Brand Comprehension

Satisfaction — Choice Criteria — Motives

Stimulus Ambiguity — Perceptual Bias

Overt Search — Attention

Significative Stimuli — Symbolic Stimuli — Social Stimuli

P plane

Observable data relating to stimuli from commercial and social environments siderably improved data-collection techniques and procedures will be needed before the full empirical potential of such models will be realized'. Ehrenberg comments: 'Stripped of the mathematics and assumptions, it does not appear that such theories contain any generalized knowledge of consumer behaviour, or that the analytic techniques have yet proved themselves in routine use'. He gives them the apt name of 'models without facts' (Ehrenberg, 1972).

Ehrenberg and repeat-buying behaviour

Ehrenberg's own work must be sharply differentiated from that of the theorists discussed already. Market statistics of choice behaviour have long existed. Purchase data for different brands is collected for successive time periods. The statistics show how many people are buying various brands in successive segments of time. Ehrenberg studied this aggregate purchase data in an attempt to discover underlying patterns and regularities. The statistics are available for many product fields to show how many people buy each brand in a market over specific given time periods (usually one month), and hence what share of the market any given brand has in a given time period, and how these shares of the market vary. Such statistics have long been the life blood of the marketing man.

Early work in the USA (Lipstein, 1959) had attempted to 'model' the shifts in brand share shown up in such statistics by using Markovian mathematics. Markov was a Russian mathematician who had developed an extension of probability theory in order to understand and predict the movement of gas particles in a container. Using the locations of particles at one point in time (State 1) and the probabilities that the gas particles would remain stationary or move at subsequent states (transitional probabilities), Markov found that he could predict the concentration of gas particles at a future point in time. Lipstein (without any very convincing success) attempted to use the same mathematics to predict movement in brand shares. The great difficulty lay of course in the specifying of transitional probabilities. What is the probability that more (or less) people will buy a certain brand of washing powder next month than bought it this month? By what means do we arrive at this transitional probability and feed it in to the Markovian

33

calculations. Markov knew the transitional probabilities of his gases; but Lipstein couldn't specify accurate transitional probabilities for the successive purchase of brands.

More and more complex mathematics have been applied to the problem, some of which use enormously cumbrous matrices, and none of which solve the central difficulty. Aaker and Morgan (1971) tried to base a mathematical model of shifts in purchases on learning theory. Stable transitional probabilities between brand purchasing patterns were not postulated, but transitional probabilities were held to depend on past learning experiences. This work has had some success in simulating market processes.

Ehrenberg has been particularly interested in what are called 'stationary markets' which data show occur very frequently. By 'stationary markets' are meant those where there is little or no change in the market over successive time periods. If a certain percentage of people buy Persil, Daz, Omo, etc., this month, it is pretty likely that the same percentages of people will buy Persil, Daz, Omo the next month. It has long been known that the best predictor of future market share for any given brand is immediate past market share.

Under the assumption of stability Ehrenberg identified two main variables.

$b =$ the proportion of the population buying brand x within some specified time period

$w =$ mean number of times buyers purchase any quantity of brand x in the same time period

(To give an example: if we are considering the soap powder market in Great Britain b would be the proportion of the population buying, say, Persil within a specified period of, say, two months; and w would be the mean number of times Persil is purchased in those same two months by any Persil purchaser.) Ehrenberg is able to show that w is a constant over all brands in any given product field. That is, the mean frequency with which Persil is bought by Persil buyers in the two month period is the same as the mean frequency with which Daz is bought by Daz buyers in the same time period etc.

Ehrenberg also goes on to show (and it is important to realize that his is an *empirical* result; it has been arrived at by examining a great mass of actual purchase data in successive time periods) that if you know the number of purchasers of a given

34

brand at Time 1, you can predict the proportion of people who will be repeat buyers in the next period and the mean number of purchases they will make. The remainder of the population (those who buy in the second time period but not the first) are held to buy with an average frequency of 1·4 units (this being a constant). So in effect all we need to know to predict repeat-buying rates in successive time periods in a stationary market is the figure w; the mean number of times buyers make any purchase of any brand in a product field at one specific time. (Bear in mind that this is held to be a constant for all brands in a product field. Daz buyers buy on average the same amount of Daz in a time period as Persil buyers do of Persil.)

This result has an undoubted elegance. But what you may ask is its use? How have we advanced our understanding of 'How people choose' by knowing how mathematically to predict repeat-purchasing rates in an aggregate level, when we have one figure of the frequency of purchase in a given observed time-period? All Ehrenberg's results are at an aggregate level. He has not been interested in following individual purchasers through from Time 1 to Time 2. He is examining only what happens to proportions of brands sold over a wide market. Can such aggregate results really illuminate processes of decision?

At the lowest they give us some facts to explain. We can look at such models as Howard and Sheth's and Engel, Kollat and Blackwell's to see if they are consonant with such regularities of purchase behaviour as Ehrenberg has empirically shown to hold in the market.

But Ehrenberg's own ingenuities of application of his laws have given them yet more interest. He can predict, using his patterns derived from 'stationary' markets, the number of repeat-buyers and average number of purchases of any brand which are to be expected in a given time period if nothing has happened to the market. This gives the marketing man a benchmark. He can assess effects of advertising, special sales, seasonal trends etc. by comparing actual data in Time 2 with predicted values. Deviations from predicted values show 'something has happened'.

There are of course dangers of circularity. If Ehrenberg's equations hold then this is a 'stationary' market, such as one would expect. If Ehrenberg's equations do not hold, then one looks for 'what has happened' . . . and it is always possible to think of explanations of 'what has happened' after the event. (Maybe the packet changed, there was a promotion, the salesmen worked harder etc.) In this sense his equations are not, I would suggest, directly 'provable'. It is difficult to think of a test one could put them to which would dis-confirm them. One's judgement of their validity must to a large extent be a pragmatic one, dependent on the conviction carried by his enormous range of examples gathered over the years. Most readers of Ehrenberg's (1974) book will, I think, find the equations persuasive, and certainly many practical marketing men have trusted them enough over the years to use them to infer the effects of special advertising pushes or of sales promotions, and to take marketing actions based on these inferences.

I have considerably over-simplified Professor Ehrenberg's results for the purpose of this short exposition. He has arrived at various other important empirical statements of repeat-purchasing behaviour. Interested readers should consult Ehrenberg, 1972 (see References).

Television viewing implications

The usefulness of Ehrenberg's laws will perhaps become clearer if we consider the work of himself and his colleagues Goodhardt and Collins on television viewing patterns (Goodhardt, Ehrenberg and Collins, 1975). The authors over many years examined repeat viewing of television programmes, and were able to show that many of the principles and mathematics developed for repeat-purchase behaviour of branded goods hold also in this field. Many cherished myths of those who schedule and design programmes were shown to be untrue. Repeat viewership of programmes held to be roughly of the same type (for instance Arts programmes) were shown to be no higher than repeat viewership of any sort of programme, predicted according to the laws of repeat viewership. There is not, then, a special small self-selected audience of 'Arts programme viewers' to be catered for as a special minority. Again this research study shows that 'minority' programmes (conceived of by the programme schedulers as produced for a special minority audience) are mainly watched by *heavy* viewers, that is by people who leave the television on for most of the evening. 'Light' viewers, the supposedly selective 'minority' audience according to the myth, actually tend most often to watch popular programmes. Programmes which are 'popular' have 'heavy viewership' precisely because they are watched both by the heavy viewers who always have the set on (even through the so-called 'minority' programmes) *and* by the light viewers who only switch the set on occasionally.

The effects of Ehrenberg's study of television viewing patterns on cherished myths have yet to percolate through to the programmers (one hopes the Annan committee responsible for rethinking the organization of broadcasting has read them). But his studies of repeat purchasing data have in their time broken up many 'marketing' myths.

Conclusion and summary

In this chapter I have briefly surveyed the kind of work carried out by academic consumer behaviour theorists. The account has necessarily been brief and selective. Three major American theories, those of Nicosia, Engel, Kollat and Blackwell and Howard and Sheth have been discussed and all have been found to suffer from untestability and lack of specificity of variables. They offer models of what consumer choice behaviour *might* be like, but offer no evidence that it is in fact like their theories.

The work of Ehrenberg in repeat purchasing behaviour has been briefly indicated and it has been concluded that though this work also is not susceptible to purely scientific testing (it is difficult to conceive how his equations could be disproved; variations in the stability of the basic equations are held to indicate 'something has happened' and *post hoc* explanations can usually be found), it does carry conviction through the sheer weight and care of the empirical work. We shall return to its effect on theorizing about 'how we choose' in Chapter 3.

2
Practitioners' theories

In the last chapter we took a look at the theories of academic consumer behaviourists as to how people choose; but it is not only academics who have addressed themselves to this problem. Politicians, ad-men, political scientists, market researchers, media-owners: none of these can proceed without some sort of working model of how people choose, and if we look into the history of the last few decades, we will find that this theory has shifted from time to time in important directions.

The 'forties, and to a large extent in this country also the 'fifties, were a time of 'issue politics'. (The Eisenhower election of 1951 was perhaps the major shift in North America to 'image' politics; but Britain lagged behind.) Politicians thought it was their job to persuade people of the value of their policies . . . to end unemployment, to set up a welfare state, or to 'set the people free'. The model was as it were 'newsy' and rational. It was assumed people choose who to vote for by deciding which policy they preferred on more or less rational and self-interested grounds.

Advertisers too believed in what they called 'news in the product'. I myself worked as a copywriter in the J. Walter Thompson of the early 'fifties. We were actually taught a way of persuading people. It was an informational approach. We were taught to look for the new promise offered by a product and to headline that, on the theory that if people only knew our product offered some advantage others didn't they would of course start buying it. I remember being asked as an exercise to prepare an advertisement for 'a fountain pen that didn't need filling'. (These were pre-Biro days and such a thing did not yet exist.) The approved headlines were all ones such as 'Now at last, the fountain pen you don't need to fill'. Anything more whimsical or indirect was deeply disapproved of. There was something called the Thompson T-square – an office mnemonic for how to plan and write advertisements. It asked us to consider WHAT message we were communicating to WHICH people in WHAT medium to WHAT end. Only when we had the answers to all these questions clear were we allowed to write our advertisements.

Underlying both the political and advertising approaches was of course an assumption that people operated rational systems of choice. They 'changed their minds', shifted from supporting one party to another because the other offered more rewarding policies; shifted from buying one product to another because the advertising showed them that the second product offered some real advantage.

This approach continued and developed in the advertising world, both in Great Britain and the United States throughout the 'fifties and into the 'sixties. Rosser Reeves' book *Reality in Advertising* was published in 1961, and summed up what was by then a very widely diffused and practised theory of how to persuade, already beginning to be slightly old-fashioned: the theory of the 'unique selling proposition'. 'Copy platforms' were routinely written in advertising agencies and these specified both the main promise to be given in any advertisement and the rationale to be given for that promise, long before any advertisement was in fact written. The 'promise' had to be unique to the product being advertised; if the product didn't have a unique selling proposition, one had to be put into its formulation. It was assumed that if a product had the right promise and the right rationale, all that had to be done was to spell it out. 'Bloggs tissue is strongest because it has a three-way weave'; 'Sheen toothpaste whitens your teeth because it has the magic ingredient XYZ'. So went the advertisements in either press or television. They were researched to test their effectiveness, but researched naively. Consumers would be asked to rate various 'propositions' for their attractiveness before any advertisements were written. After the advertisements were written and published, tests would be carried out to see if they had been read and remembered. Success was held to be achieved if a significant proportion of customers could remember both promise and rationale: 'Bloggs tissue is strongest because it has a three way weave'. It was unusual for anyone to investigate whether those who remembered the advertisement also bought the product.

But the 'sixties faith in these hectoring and rationalistic methods of persuasion had crumbled, under attacks from two sides, from the world of sociological theory and the world of Freudian and post-Freudian theory.

The sociological attack had most effect in mass media and politics. The work of the Michigan school of researchers was particularly effective. Theorists from the 1950s had been collecting data to show that people did not in fact appear to 'change their mind' very often as to how they would vote. It was argued that the major effect on voting patterns was the way one's parents and neighbours voted. Results were produced to show that most people voted like their parents anyway, that perhaps the model of 'floating voters' waiting to be persuaded was radically misguided. Instead, one must think of a large body of voters with ready-made tribal loyalties – be they to Democrats or Republicans, Labour or Conservative – which were virtually unchangeable by any political effort. Only a few strange creatures in the middle were actually rootless enough to be able to 'change their minds'.

This theory had a vast effect on political behaviour. Politicians increasingly saw their task as that of 'getting out' their own tribal vote. It wasn't really worth arguing to the public about issues or trying to educate them about the advantages of one policy as against another. It was not believed that an electoral campaign could actually change people's views; these were considered fixed by their lifetime's experience. Politicians stopped arguing much in public; and addressed themselves more and more to calling up the tribal loyalties of 'our people'. They had ceased to believe in the possibility of messages and communications affecting voting patterns much in any way.

Advertisers became equally cynical about the possibilities of rational persuasion of the need for 'reason-why'. Part of the reason was the purely technical one of the vast shift to the television medium, which, of its nature, is better able to communicate pictures than words, images than arguments; biased, some would say, against understanding. But tele-

40

vision's purely technical bias against understanding can be exaggerated. A medium is also how we use it. More influential was the belated discovery by advertisers of the work of motivational and psychodynamic researchers. Dichter is a key name here. His first studies were carried out in the United States in 1939.

Dichter had trained as an analytic psychologist in Vienna, and in the United States of the 'forties and 'fifties had an enormous fashionable effect in applying theories based on Freudian insights about the unconscious to marketing behaviour. Men were held to choose convertibles because they wanted a wife not a mistress; women to dislike cakemixes because they felt the need to contribute their own efforts to the sacred task of cake-making . . . and so on, and so on. (Vance Packard's book *The Hidden Persuaders* (1957) gives a vast range of amusing examples of this now out-dated approach.)

Yet another influence on advertising theory and practice was the work of David Ogilvy who invented the term 'brand image'. Ogilvy reminded advertisers that no individual message stood alone; that consumers already had a defined picture of a brand, based on its physical reality and past history. Every attempt should be made, Ogilvy argued, to bear this image in mind when writing an advertisement and try to move it in a more positive direction. The strength of his approach was his emphasis on elements other than factual information and rational argument in advertisements. The associations raised by an advertisement were seen to be of importance. It is associations and memories that make up an image (see A6).

So the 'seventies find the world of the commercial or political persuaders as full of contradictory intuitions as we found the world of academics. No one appears to have a very clear idea of how choice is made. They only know it is complex. Perhaps the researchers have the most formalized and clear models of anyone. They are often asked to explore the patterns and mechanisms of choice. You cannot study a subject without having at least an implicit model of how it works. What models are the researchers using?

The market research world is as open to fashion and new ideas as any other, but I think most researchers practising today would agree that there are really two main methods used when studies of the motivations for choice are called for.

These methods are often referred to as 'quantitative' and 'qualitative' studies.

Quantified studies and the correlational method

The kind of 'quantified' study which is carried out can vary widely in detail. But one particular technique which I shall describe here is widely spread through Europe and North America. The marketing man who goes to a research agency in Europe or the States and asks for a 'quantified' study of attitudes and behaviour, or a study of the reasons for buying, will probably get something of this sort.

Firstly, a long list of attributes of the brand to be studied and of competing brands in the same product-field will be generated. The brand may be a kind of soap or detergent; it may be a political party; it could be a broadcasting station. The attribute list is generated in various ways; sometimes through 'group discussions', which consist of groups of consumers sitting and talking about brands while their words are tape-recorded and lists later made of attributes of brands they have mentioned. Sometimes the lists are prepared by marketing men from commonsense or from their knowledge. Sometimes elaborate procedures such as 'Kelly grids' (see F1) are used to generate descriptions in consumer language of qualities which discriminate one brand from another. The list of attributes generated is usually found to be too long and too diverse to use entire in a quantified survey. So the next stage of the research is to reduce the list, and the favoured method of doing this is by factor analysis. All the dimensions or attributes which have been identified at the first stage are included in a questionnaire and a small sample of the public is asked to scale the items. They all have to fill in a long list of questions, scaling such statements as 'Persil has lots of lather', 'Persil was used by my mother', 'Persil smells nice', etc. on a scale running from *very true*, through *quite true*, *slightly true*, *inbetween*, *slightly false*, *quite false* to *very false*. The same list of attributes will be scaled for every brand. Once this has been done, a factor analysis is carried out to find which items co-vary. The factor analysis will settle typically on a four or five factor solutions. That is, four or five groups of items will be arrived at; within each group, response to any item is relatively predictable, given that response to the others is known. A final questionnaire is produced which includes about two items from each factor. A considerable portion of the total variance is usually thrown away (as 'unimportant' factors or 'little' factors). Then a final survey is carried out with the short list of attributes. Criterion measures, sometimes of past behaviour, sometimes of overall attitude to a brand, sometimes of behavioural intention are included in the questionnaire. The computer is asked to discover which item on the attribute list, or which 'factor' on the attribute list, co-varies most with one or all of the criterion measures. It is then assumed that the items which co-vary most with the chosen criterion measure(s) are the most 'important' items for choice. Lists are drawn up which will say things like: 'The most important factor affecting choice of washing powder for the heavy wash is a belief that the powder washes whitest, the second most important factor is a belief in the powder's cleaning power, the third most important factor is price.' Out of this kind of result is marketing and advertising policy made.

Now this procedure is widely spread (with many variations) and its practitioners tend to think of it as atheoretic. They would deny that they are operating from a particular model of choice behaviour. They are just technicians doing dispassionate research, according to the best professional models.

But in fact the procedure outlined is riddled with assumptions about the nature of consumer behaviour, all of which could be questioned.

An initial assumption is that all attributes which a consumer can perceive about a particular object of choice are relevant to her choice. Pains are usually taken to make the initial list of attributes selected as inclusive and wide as possible. There may be lists of as many as 100 attributes. Intellectual completion is aimed for. The 'Kelly grid' procedure frequently used by British market researchers can elicit enormous lists of attributes from a consumer.

Next it is assumed that if attributes co-vary (that is, if a consumer who scales one high is likely to scale another, different attribute high) they will be in some way measuring the same dimension; that consumers are in general only influenced by four or five large factors (that is bundles of co-varying items), and that the small factors can safely be neglected. It is quite routine in these studies for the 'factors' selected for the final questionnaire to cover only about half of the variance of the items measured in the pilot questionnaire. Many items which have no co-varying items are thrown out of the study. Yet they may have no co-variants, simply because paucity of language means they have not occurred in the initial pilot survey in many synonymous forms. I have seen a shampoo survey in which 'scent' fell out as a measurable factor – because there are not, in fact, many synonyms for describing scent.

Finally, and most importantly, it is assumed that 'factors' or even items which co-vary with some criterion measure are necessarily 'important' to choice. Yet with part of our minds we all know that correlation is not cause (see A8). Someone once showed that the number of double whiskies a man drinks after dinner, co-varies very well with the number of pounds a year over £8,000 he earns. But no-one thinks he earns the extra money *because* he consumes the double whiskies. (We have really learnt nothing about cause, though we may have found a pointer to an underlying connection – if we could identify it.) Social scientists may discover that the best predictor of a person's socio-economic class at thirty is the 'stream' they were placed in at school. It is not thus proved that the streaming at school is the cause, or even an important cause, of class stratification.

Even this cursory examination of the 'routine' market research model shows that it is full of assumptions. There is an implicit model of consumers processing a great and inclusive number of 'beliefs' or 'attributes' of different choice-objects, but only those which hang together in co-varying groups actually influencing them; and of there being a very direct relationship indeed between the extent the consumers go along with these actual beliefs and what they finally do or choose. None of these assumptions are proven; indeed there is considerable evidence (to which I shall return) that they are all wrong. We do not know that all beliefs about a choice object are important to the choice process, we do not know that single isolated beliefs which do not co-vary with others are of no importance, we do not know that correlations with behaviour past or future or with attitude is necessarily causative.

A model of consumer behaviour is being assumed in practice by this market research model and it is one for which there is very little evidence.

The same total lack of evidence as to validity is true of the other major market research model in use in Europe and North America; the motivation research model (see D2). In market research parlance 'motivation research' means sets of group discussions and/or depth interviews, often monitored by trained psychologists, sometimes monitored by people who have taught themselves this speciality. The 'group discussant' or interviewer will usually talk to two, three or four groups of seven to ten people at a time, and as result of these discussions (often tape- or video-recorded) write up a report on the views and 'motivations' of the average consumer. No attempt is made to content-analyse the group discussion in any formal way. The discussant-reporter relies on his informal ability to summarize the main lines of discussion and the main points raised. Sometimes the discussant-reporter limits himself to describing views which he has found 'out there' among his tiny sample of consumers. More often he goes further than this and speculates on 'underlying' motivations which are affecting the consumers' attitudes and behaviour. It is on the description or inference of these 'underlying' motives that the trained psychologist comes in useful. Psychologists have a great range of descriptive concepts, ranging from those of Freud, to concepts such as need achievement or desire for conformity, which it is easy to see operating in any given group. The psychologist is rarely at a loss to pick out *some* 'underlying motivation'. And proof of course is not required. A bright hunch is all that is needed.

The hidden assumption, of course, of the whole method is that consumers themselves cannot understand their own behaviour. It is not based on motives which are present to their own minds; otherwise one could simply ask them what those motives were. They may *claim* to be buying a car because it is the right price for them, their wife likes it or it has good mileage and power. But *actually* a skilled observer can discern, by the exercise of his arcane knowledge, the *real* underlying reason why the customer is attracted to that car; the reasons that are inaccessible to the consumers' minds.

Current fashions in the use of 'synectic' groups reflect exactly the same underlying model. The consumer is thought of as having two parts to his mind; a conscious or rationalizing part which can answer survey questions and an 'unconscious' or 'autistic' part which can only be reached by projective techniques, drawings and acting out. It is held that it is the 'unconscious' inaccessible motives which are the influential ones.

Once again, one can only comment that there is very little validating evidence for this model, any more than there is for the 'quantification' type of market research described earlier. Both are making assumptions about consumer behaviour; assumptions which have not been put to scientific test.

Conclusion and summary

In this chapter we have surveyed briefly the models used by practising advertising men, politicians and market researchers as to 'how we choose'. These models have no more claim to a purely scientific validity than those discussed in Chapter 1, but are of interest in showing the number of contradictory ways in which the processes of choice are modelled.

3
Consumer behaviour and the market: some myths and theories

It is not only advertising men, persuaders and politicians who have held theories of consumer choice. Economists too have always known that if they are to model the processes of the market, they must make some assumptions about individual methods of choice and decision. The traditional model of economic man can be traced back to Adam Smith and Jeremy Bentham; Adam Smith based his doctrine of economic growth on the principle that man is motivated by self-interest. Bentham conceived of man as weighing the pleasures and pains of every possible action on a fine hedonic calculus, pursuing what gives him the greatest pleasure and the least pain. Marshall introduced the concept of money as the measuring rod of all value. In classical economics man maximizes his utilities; every market decision a man makes is made so as to maximize economic gain to himself.

Thorstein Veblen was one of the earliest economists to modify this picture. In his *The Theory of the Leisure Class* (1899) Veblen shows how much of economic life is motivated not by intrinsic needs or by maximization of monetary gain but by a search for pleasure and status. Veblen invented the term 'conspicuous consumption' and showed how much economic behaviour was influenced by a desire to 'show off', to display the high status and power brought by wealth. He himself had been influenced by the new science of social anthropology, and was very aware of the need to allow into theories of choice behavioural factors which could not be measured solely by the measuring rod of money. Man is controlled also by the desire to gain status in his group, to fit in with his friends, by the norms and habits of his society.

Today, surrounded as we are by the confusion of so much classical economics in the face of inflation and unemployment, there is a new realization of the need for a more sophisticated micro-economics and for more plausible theories of how choice factors are operating at the individual and atomistic level. George Katona in the United States pioneered the use of direct studies of individual's expectations and intentions in the forecasting of economic trends, and Katona's work has inspired a whole school of studies on the behavioural and psychological basis of economic trends. Katona has shown how individual psychological changes (changes in attitude for instance or in buying intentions) can, when aggregated, have both an explanatory and predictive function for the movements of the market. If a significantly high proportion of the population is optimistic and hopeful of future prosperity, the market will behave in quite a different way from the way it behaves when shrinking incomes and disaster are the expectation. Economists have become aware of the influence of individual expectations on such end results as the processes of saving and hence of investment, and the management of inflation. The simplistic myth of rational 'economic' man is seen not to be enough, and theoreticians are searching for ways of quantifying and handling individual beliefs and expectations at the micro-economic level. It is becoming clear that without this micro-economic understanding we are unlikely to be able to solve the problems of late capitalist society.

The break up of the marketing myth

Marketing men too have been becoming dissatisfied with their simple pictures of how men choose. John Treasure of J. Walter Thompson (a major advertising company) has recently described the classic 'marketing myth' as follows:

I think you will agree that in most discussions of brand advertising people inside and outside advertising take it for granted that its chief purpose is to increase the sales of a brand and that it does so by converting non-users of the brand into users of it . . . or, in other words, by persuading people to switch their purchases from Brand A to Brand B. Many advertising people it seems to me, have a kind of picture in their minds (or a model, if you prefer the term) in which housewives appear as being either loyal or disloyal. There are those housewives who fall in love with Brand A or with Brand B and stay totally loyal to it and there are those who have a series of short-lived but passionate love affairs with Brand A, then Brand B, then Brand C and so on. These are the Brand switchers, whose attention somehow or other the advertiser has to attract. (Treasure, 1975)

Examination of purchasing data has made this model out-of-date. Treasure presents a table (Table 3.1), which shows that in most product fields housewives buy more than one brand. She has a 'brand repertoire', and probably has two or three brands in the house at any one moment. The reason may be that different products meet different sub-needs or serve different people; she may choose Persil for the heavy wash, Dreft for hand washing, Imperial Leather toilet soap for Dad, Camay for Mum, Johnson's Baby soap for the children. The reason may be that the housewife is buying for convenience or money off; Tesco Orange Squash this week, Marks and Spencers the next. Whatever the reason, the fact is well established that multi-brand purchasing is the general rule. The picture of housewives as regular purchasers of one brand, under persuasion or conversion switching to another has been, the data shows, quite wrong.

How does a brand grow?

An argument has ensued about how brands do in fact grow, how changes in the market happen. Andrew Ehrenberg has reminded us that the normal position of any market is stability without great change, yet it is undeniable that brands do wax and wane, grow in popularity over the years or die. Change may be gradual but it occurs. One particular theoretic argument has centred round whether the growth of a brand (its rise in sales) occurs through increasing penetration (more and more people buying it) or through increasing frequency of purchase (the same people buying it more often). If one or the

Table 3.1 The proportion of users who use more than one brand (Treasure, 1975)

Product Field	Universe of Users	% of users using more than one brand.
Butter and margarine	Housewives	87%
Sweets in tubes and for children	Adults	79%
Breakfast cereals (cold)	Housewives	77%
Bottled beers, stouts and lagers	Adults	71%
Canned fruit	Housewives	71%
Meat and vegetable extracts	Housewives	69%
Chocolate bars	Adults	67%
Chocolate assortments	Adults	65%
Toilet soap	Housewives	65%
Cheese	Housewives	64%
Washing powders etc. (for clothes and fabric)	Housewives	64%
Wrapped bread	Housewives	59%
Cigarettes	Adults	58%
Jam	Housewives	56%
Chocolate biscuits	Housewives	56%
Fruit squashes and cordials	Housewives	55%
Eye make-up	Women	55%
Canned soup	Housewives	54%
Lavatory cleansers and domestic bleaches	Housewives	54%
Yoghurt	Housewives	54%
Toilet paper	Housewives	53%
Shoe polish	Housewives	53%
Scouring powders and pastes	Housewives	53%
Frozen peas and other vegetables	Housewives	52%
Facial tissues	Adults	51%
Flour	Housewives	50%

Table 3.1 continued

Product Field	Universe of Users	% of users using more than one brand.
Cakes and sponge mixes	Housewives	49%
Instant coffee	Housewives	49%
Headache remedies and analgesics	Adults	47%
Lipstick	Women	47%
Shampoos	Men	46%
Make-up (including foundation)	Women	46%
Hair sprays and lacquer	Women	45%
Fruit juice and vegetable juice	Adults	45%
Tomato ketchup	Housewives	43%
Tea (by the packet)	Housewives	43%
Hand creams and lotions	Women	41%
Suntan lotions, oils and creams	Women	40%
Tea bags	Housewives	37%
Indigestion remedies	Adults	37%
Breakfast cereals (hot)	Housewives	36%
Razor blades	Men	35%
Shaving cream	Men	35%
Health and vitamin drinks and syrups	Housewives	34%
Carpet cleaners	Housewives	28%
Honey	Housewives	28%
Laxatives and salts	Adults	28%
Household soaps	Housewives	26%
Pastry	Housewives	25%
Starch	Housewives	17%

Source: Target Group Index (Great Britain) 1973

other theory could be shown to be true, we would have learned something about the mechanisms of choice, and the marketing men would have learned something about how to go about increasing sales.

Ehrenberg's equation had suggested that it is the penetration of a brand (b in his equation: the proportion of the total population buying brand X in any given period) which is the crucial variable. After all Ehrenberg considers w (the rate of frequency of purchase in any given time period) to be a constant both over time and in any given product field. Ehrenberg has specifically argued that increased sales arise essentially through increased brand penetration, not through increasing sales frequencies. Treasure, on the other hand, suggests that frequency of purchase (Ehrenberg's w) may be the crucial variable. He writes:

> The task of advertising is not primarily one of conversion but rather of reinforcement and reassurance . . . sales of a given brand may be increased without converting to the brand any new consumers, but merely by inducing its existing users . . . those who already use it at least occasionally . . . to use it more frequently. (Treasure, 1975)

Treasure suggests that the opposition between himself and Ehrenberg may be more apparent than real, and to do with the time-scale used to develop equations (this suggestion was first made by Corlett, ADMAP 1974). Changes in sales over one day periods are going to depend more on b (penetration: proportion of total population buying) than on w (the average frequency of purchase) because w is bound to be constant if one considers two successive days. Each product is unlikely to be bought more than once a day; but different people are going to buy on successive days. On the other hand if one thinks of time periods of a year, it is unlikely that either b (penetration) or w (frequency of purchase) will change; but slightly more likely that b will change from one year to the next than w if sufficiently large aggregates are considered. A moment's reflection will show why. w (frequency of rate of purchase) over a large population is bound to remain pretty constant for most products. There is little variation in the amount of soap powder or tea or jam households are likely to consume from year to year, and little variation in the distribution of single or large families over a whole sample. One cannot expect the mean frequency of rate of purchase of a particular brand to vary much from year to year. Even b (the penetration of the brand; the number of people who have ever tried it) is unlikely to vary much when successive year-long time periods are considered. The penetration figures will include even the occasional purchasers. Some of them may have moved into being more frequent purchasers but this will not affect the penetration total.

Corlett's hypothesis

Corlett, in the article referred to above, has been one of the few people to use empirical sales data to attempt to investigate the *cause* of the growth of a brand, rather than to predict movements in the market. In an investigation of the milk drinks market in Great Britain, Corlett showed that users of large-selling brands in this field, tended to buy more of their total purchases in that field (to 'solus' or 'major' users) in the big brand concerned. Or to put it another way, users of large brands (big-selling brands with large brand share) tend to comprise a higher proportion of people using only that brand and none other in the market. Figure 3.1, reproduced from Corlett's paper, shows how the proportion of 'solus' or 'major' users of a brand increases with penetration. He comments:

If the relationship between large and small brands may be interpreted in terms of a process of growth, it will be seen from the diagram that the reason why the proportion of 'solus' or 'major' users among a brand's users (the hatched portion of the brands) increases with penetration is that the brand does not begin to acquire 'solus' or 'major' users immediately on its entry into the market, but a little later (as illustrated by the solid line in the diagram leaving the base-line a little to the right of the origin), which makes sense. (Corlett, 1974)

The interesting thing about Corlett's data is that it suggests neither the 'reinforcement' nor the 'conversion' theories are in themselves totally true about brand growth. Just as common-sense would suggest, brands grow partly through attracting quite new buyers (increasing their penetration levels, making new converts) and partly through increased frequency of use

53

among existing users, typically at the expense of less popular brands. (Users of a major brand are more likely to turn into solus or major users of that brand.)

If one speculates as to the causes of both these processes, there is little reason to think them dissimilar. Existing users grow to use their brand more frequently. This has been called

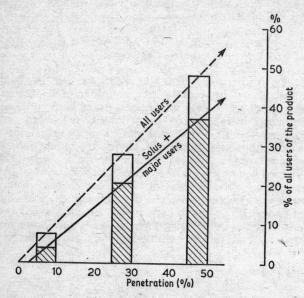

Fig. 3.1 *How the proportion of 'solus' or 'major' users increases with penetration* (Corlett, 1974)

'reinforcement'; whatever reinforcement is, it implies some growth in satisfaction with the use of the product. Non-users start to use the product. This has been called 'conversion'. Whatever conversion is, it implies some growth in the belief that using the product will give satisfaction. It is difficult to see why the two processes should ever have been put in opposition. We are ignorant of the exact mechanism of either. But the commonsense probability that either will be related to some increase in expected satisfaction levels seems exactly similar.

The marketing man's conflict between 'reinforcement' theory and 'conversion' theory seems largely, then, an artificial one. It probably arose in the first place through a tendency to put too much causal weight on Ehrenberg's equations (which, I have argued, though predictively useful depend for their relationship between penetration and frequency of purchase on the time periods at which the measures are taken), combined with a spill-over from controversies extant in the 'fifties and 'sixties in the field of political behaviour and media studies.

In the 1940s attitude change had been studied (largely by the Yale school) in terms which suggested that people could and might 'change their minds', that individual factors of belief and conviction were relevant to action. In the 'fifties and 'sixties the pendulum swung the other way. Theorists such as Klapper (1960) and Lazarsfeld (1948) presented data suggesting that most voters voted the way their parents voted; most users of the media attended to messages which 'reinforced' their existing convictions and neglected other messages; that most people were in some sense creatures of their own sociological conditioning, not so much free men engaged in choice, as conditioned creatures responding accordingly to their sociological circumstance. In the 'fifties and 'sixties it was the fashionable thing to say that men did not choose, were not converted, but simply went on much as they and their parents always had, and that the only thing media messages could do for them was to 'reinforce' their original conviction. It is not surprising that this fashionable point of view spilled over into consumer behaviour theory and marketing theory, where it is still flourishing.

Political behaviour studies were particularly influential in presenting a picture of a citizen not open to persuasion. Campbell, Converse, Miller and Stokes (1960) in probably the most influential single study of voting behaviour yet written, drew an unflattering picture of 'the American voter'. According to these authors the American voter was an apathetic, uninformed individual who had developed an attachment to a political party (largely because his or her family was attached to that party) and who tended to vote for the candidate of that party, paying little attention to the issues of the campaign, having no real conception of the differences between the parties, and little or no political ideology.

Following in the footsteps of their American colleagues, Butler and Stokes (1969) found relatively few differences between the British voter and the American voter. Indeed, if anything, the British voter is seen as even more firmly entrenched in a party alignment, and this 'party identification' or 'partisanship' serves as the central explanatory concept in their analysis of voting behaviour.

Politicians in their turn have been greatly influenced by these political behaviour analyses, and in the 'sixties and early 'seventies the task of the politician at an election was seen largely as one of 'getting our people out'. However the 'seventies have seen growing doubts about this type of analysis of the situation. The pendulum at last seems to be swinging the other way. Both in the USA and Great Britain, evidence has been brought to light which suggests voters may be more responsive to issues, less dependent on early socialization and current reinforcement, than the 'sixties theorists thought. The Butler and Stokes analysis does not explain important features of the British electoral scene in the last ten years, such as the increased fluctuation in voting, the decrease in turnout and the decreasing share of the electorate accounted for by the sum of the supporters of the major parties. The inability of Butler and Stokes's model to predict such important features of the British scene is discussed at length by Crewe (1974) who has reanalysed some of Butler and Stokes's data to show that while self-reported party allegiance to the three major British parties has apparently been increasing since the war, these parties have in the last decade been increasingly rejected at the polls. The 'Michigan' model of Campbell, Converse, Miller and Stokes cannot account for the apparent steady erosion of commitment to these parties. In the USA Fishbein and Coombes (1974) have recently reported data suggesting that the American voter is a relatively well-informed, intelligent decision maker, who is aware of the differences between candidates and parties and who uses the information available to him to make a rational choice at the polls. Similar results for the United Kingdom have recently been presented by Fishbein, Thomas and Jaccard (1976).

Doubts are being thrown on the purely sociological model of choice behaviour in the political and media fields. Perhaps the time is ripe too to consider in the marketing field whether consumers may not sometimes exercise 'choice'.

I would like to suggest that neither in politics, media studies nor in marketing would theories of 'reinforcement' or 'conversion' be seen as in opposition. Clearly men's habits and choices are influenced by the whole of their past learning experience. This can be mediated through the social environment in which they live, through their parents and friends. But the possibilities of change exist and must not be neglected. We ourselves seem to have the experience of making choices which are not fully predetermined. Such choices are probably also made by others, in the books they read, the way they vote, the brands they choose to purchase. This book is a study of the process of choice. It does not attempt to deny that much of that choice will be constrained by environmental and sociological factors. But it does suggest that the role of conscious, volitional choice is a real one, and one whose processes are worth studying.

Part Two
TOWARDS A NEW PSYCHOLOGICAL THEORY

So far I have argued that we believe that both we ourselves and others have some capacity for choice. We can 'change our minds' about what products we buy, what television programmes we watch, what means of transport we use, whom we wish to live with. Of course, all these choices are constrained to some extent by outside factors; but we have at least some capacity to make choices between different alternatives, despite the constraints.

Marketing men, advertising men, consumer behaviour theorists, all have models of how these choices are made; but none we have examined so far carry any great conviction. Most are 'models without facts' and proceed by naming variables, rather than suggesting ways of isolating or measuring them. These models may be interesting mental exercises, but they are untestable and can have no status as science. Some theorists have argued that most behaviour is stationary and traditional; we need no model of choice, for only the reinforcement of existing behaviour is relevant. I have attempted to disentangle these concepts of reinforcement and stationarity, and have argued that the marketing theory debate as to whether 'penetration' (number of people buying in any time period) or 'repeat purchase' (number of purchases made by an individual in a given time period) is the key variable in change or growth of a brand, dissolves when one realizes that we can get different equations depending on the length of the given time period. I have also argued that the media theorists and marketing men's dichotomy between 'conversion' and 'reinforcement' dissolves when one realizes that both processes are essentially processes of becoming more rather than less likely to choose one among several alternatives. The irreducible question remains. How do we become more likely to make one choice rather than another? None of the consumer behaviour theorists have helped us. In this part we shall see what psychology has to offer.

4
Towards an attitude theory

In a sense all of psychology is relevant to theories of choice. Classical learning theory is an attempt to account for why we do what we do in terms of a few simple learning mechanisms (see A3). Group theory and conformity theory attempt to sort out how much of what we do is controlled by our peers and our environment (B2). Theories of language behaviour and cognitive theories attempt to understand the underlying thought processes which affect all behaviour including choice behaviour (A7). But the area of psychology which has traditionally concentrated on explicating relationships between inner variables and behaviour, is attitude theory (B3).

Any book or chapter, or article on attitude theory will make heavy weather of defining the attitude concept. An enormous variety of different definitions have been offered. But in the almost one hundred years in which attitude studies have continued, a certain consensus about what is being studied has emerged. Most investigators would agree that attitude can be described as 'a learned predisposition to respond in a consistently favourable or unfavourable manner with respect to a given object'. Fishbein and Ajzen (1972) identified no less than 500 different operations which had been used as measures of attitudes, but even this wide variety of measuring instruments all assumed that attitudes are learned, that they are in some sense a predisposition to behave, and that they have something to do with an evaluative dimension (that is with whether the person who holds the attitude is 'for' or 'against' the attitude object).

Despite superficial disagreements there is thus some consensus in psychologists' definition of 'attitude'.

The first thing to note is that we cannot necessarily *assume* that attitudes as so defined exist. It is the psychologists who have hypothesized that these 'learned predispositions to respond in a favourable or unfavourable direction' do in some sense exist, and have stuck with the hypothesis for nearly a hundred years of study and research. What evidence have they for the reality of their concept?

The main evidence lies in measurement work. Especially in the 'twenties and 'thirties of this century, a lot of the work in the attitude area circled round attempts to measure with reliability and validity this hypothetical underlying variable, the 'attitude'. Thurstone, Likert, Osgood, Guttmann all devoted years of research effort to devising 'attitude scales'; ways in which the hypothesized 'attitudes' could be measured. The result of all their work is undeniably to show that *something* exists which can be measured with reliability on attitude scales. Again and again the measurement theorists have shown that they can range a population on an evaluative scale for or against an object with a high degree of test–re-test reliability. The kinds of measures used are described briefly in B3, *Values, Attitudes and Behaviour Change*, though for a fuller account readers are referred to Oppenheim (1966) or Fishbein (1967).

Essentially most of them depend on paper and pencil tests. The subject of the attitude scale is asked to check his agreement or disagreement with a statement or a series of statements about the attitude object. His answers are given numerical weights and collated. Undoubtedly the techniques which have been developed can come up with replicable results for individuals and populations.

But what are these measures measuring? The problem is similar to that which measurement theorists have found with the IQ scales. The Intelligence Quotient is clearly a measure of something; but whether it is a measure of anything normally described by a non-psychologist as 'intelligence' is an altogether deeper question. Many theorists would argue that IQ scales are only a measure of whatever it is IQ scales measure. The same may be true of attitude scales. The extent and width of their use shows that they are measuring *something*; there is an underlying hypothetical variable which our attitude measurement techniques have identified and can measure. But can we be certain that these paper and pencil tests really are measuring 'a learned pre-disposition to respond in a favourable or unfavourable direction towards a given attitude object'?

There are at least three separate problems:

(a) How do we know this measured hypothetical underlying variable is indeed a predisposition to respond in a certain way? Has it anything to do with behaviour at all? Can we show it has any connection with behaviour?

(b) How do we know this measured underlying hypothetical variable has anything to do with learning experience? Can we show that it depends on learning? Where does the 'attitude' come from, what is it based on? Have we any evidence?

(c) How do we know that this underlying variable we are measuring with our 'attitude' measuring techniques does not simply depend on behaviour? Perhaps it is just a disguised measure of behaviour? Not a 'pre-disposition to respond' at all but simply a reflection of the last behavioural response?

These three problems will each be considered separately.

The attitude concept and behaviour

Throughout the history of attitude studies psychologists have tried to show that their measurable variable 'attitude' really does relate to behaviour. After all it was in an attempt to understand the roots of behaviour that the attitude concept was first developed. Interest in it was sustained because it was hoped it would be an underlying explicatory variable for variations in behaviour.

Unfortunately the attempts to show a clear relationship between attitudes and behaviour have not been very successful. To United Kingdom readers the most accessible summary of the relevant research is contained in *Attitudes and Behaviour* edited by Kerry Thomas (1971). This text reprints, among other articles, a classic review of the relevant research by Wicker (1969) in which he concludes on the basis of a careful examination of all the studies then extant: 'It is considerably more likely that attitudes will be unrelated or only slightly related to overt behaviours than that attitudes will be closely related to actions'. Again and again psychologists carefully measure attitudes according to the best techniques; then compare the attitude scores with some behaviour related to the attitude object and find only small or insignificant correlations. Most of the work up till the 1970s fails to substantiate any real relationship between measured attitudes and behaviour. The psychologists believe they are measuring a predisposition to respond when they measure attitude and occasional relationships are found, but there is certainly no one-to-one relationship between attitude measures and subsequent behaviour.

The attitude concept and learning experience

We are on rather stronger ground with our second question: how can we be certain that our measured 'attitude' has anything to do with learning experience? Attitude is measured through the responses to paper and pencil tests. Typically the subject checks whether he agrees or disagrees with certain specific statements and how strongly he agrees or disagrees. If the attitude to the Communist party is under scrutiny, he may be asked to say if he agrees that the Communist party is under the control of Moscow, is tyrannical, is un-democratic, has many or few supporters. It is clear from the very nature of the measuring instruments used that 'attitude' (whatever it may be) is related to and dependent on underlying 'beliefs'. Whatever these beliefs are they are at the least links made between various objects and various other objects, they are predications about objects, they are statements of probability. However we describe the beliefs, it is clear that they are not innate, they must at some time have been learned. 'Attitude' is undoubtedly a learned predisposition, even if we must remain uncertain as to what it predisposes.

Do attitudes depend on behaviour?

Our third question is the possible dependence of the attitude measure on behaviour. It has been explained above that attitude is far from being a clear predictor of future behaviour, but perhaps it is dependent on or subsequent to past behaviour? The suggestion has been particularly raised by a group of attitude theorists known as the cognitive dissonance school (see B1, B3). Some experiments carried out by this school showed that, at least in certain cases, attitude measures would change over time to fit behaviour 'dissonant' with the original attitude. Thus if a person initially in favour of a given point of view (with a measured favourable attitude to it) was induced to write an essay supporting the opposite point of view, his 'attitude' would change after the 'dissonant' act of writing the counter-attitudinal essay, and come more in line with the attitude of the essay. The dissonance theorists also showed that if someone were given a large reward for performing a counter-attitudinal act, they were *less* likely to change their attitude towards the act than if they were given a small reward. This result, they suggested, showed that the mechanism at work was not a simple one of subjects 'changing their mind' as a result of more information, or a reward being offered for a positive response to a previously disliked object. The people who got a *small* reward, changed more than those who got a big reward. The dissonance experiments were carefully set up to attempt to show that acting contrary to one's attitude *in itself* (without any extraneous factors of more information or more reward) changed the initial attitude. The explanation offered by the dissonance theorists was that men could not stand finding themselves inconsistent; they get uncomfortable if doing something they know they disapprove of. They are motivated to remove the dissonance, and since they cannot undo an act, they simply change an attitude.

Dissonance theory has many lacunae, and fails in the end (for me, at any rate) to carry conviction. Of late, researchers are finding it more and more difficult to replicate the results in any consistent way; nor does the concept of an inbuilt 'drive' towards consistency look quite as attractive now as when it was first propounded. However, the dissonance theorists do raise the important possibility that attitudes change to fit in with behaviour, rather than any causative chain working in the opposite direction; and this point must be remembered when we consider the relevance of attitude theory to an understanding of choice behaviour. If 'attitudes' are simply a measured reflection of past choices, then they can go no further in explaining future choice than can the past choices themselves.

For the purposes of this book, we are interested in psychological attitude theory only in so far as it can shed light on choice behaviour. So far, what I have said may appear depressing. We have learned that psychologists can measure with some consistency, something that they have agreed to call 'attitudes' and which they define as 'a learned predisposition to respond in a consistently favourable or unfavourable manner to a given attitude object'. If we could be confident of the existence of such a variable defined in such a way, we would indeed be on the lines to an understanding of choice behaviour. However, we find that though we can indeed have confidence that psychologists can measure something called 'attitudes' and that these 'attitudes' depend on past learning experience, there is little clear evidence that attitudes so measured do genuinely predict behaviour (or, as we might put it, 'choice'); and that some theorists have suspected that the attitude concept as measured does not itself predict or predispose towards certain choices, but may be itself a residual of past choices.

It must here be noted that the lack of a clear one-to-one relationship between measured attitudes and measured behaviour which was documented by Wicker and discussed above, not only shows that attitude is not itself a simple indicator of subsequent choice; it also shows that attitude is not a simple resultant of past choice.

'Attitudes' exist; sometimes the measures of them show some faint relationship to behaviour past or future. They are learned mental constructs which can be measured with some reliability. Psychologists have always had an obstinate feeling that they have *something* to do with subsequent behaviour; that has been the source of the interest in them. By introspection and commonsense we suspect that 'attitudes' have something to do with our behaviour; but until the last decade or so no-one has been able to come up with a convincing demonstration of such a relationship, or a convincing theory of what the relationship might be.

However, a theory has recently become available. It can be described as expectancy-value theory and will be discussed in the next chapter.

5
Expectancy-value theory

Our discussion so far has shown the need for some definitions. We have seen that psychologists define attitude as 'a learned predisposition to respond in a consistently favourable or unfavourable direction towards a given attitude object', but we have also seen that the actual evidence for relationship of attitudes towards any consistent response is in fact thin. For the moment, therefore, I would suggest defining 'attitudes' as 'that which is measured by attitudinal measures of the type devised by Likert, Thurstone, Osgood and Guttmann. The placing of individuals on an over-all evaluative scale with regard to a given attitude object.'

For this definition to be meaningful a word or two more must be said about attitude scaling. There is strong and irrefutable evidence that attitudes as measured by the scales named, do in fact correlate with each other very highly indeed. Shaw and Wright (1967) and Robinson and Shaver (1969) have reported reliability coefficients for a large variety of Likert, Thurstone, Guttmann and semantic differential scales. Whenever investigators have obtained more than one measure of attitude towards the same object, the results were almost always identical. For example Edwards and Kenney (1946) constructed Thurstone and Likert scales to measure attitudes towards the church. These different measures were found to be highly correlated. Similarly Osgood, Suci and Tannenbaum (1957) compared their semantic differential measure of attitude towards crop rotation with a Guttmann scale designed to measure attitudes towards the same object. Again these two techniques yielded comparable results. There is abundant evidence for the equivalence of different measures of attitude towards the same object. All scales come up with one single number for each subject which names the position of the subject towards the attitude object on an evaluative dimension.

It therefore seems reasonable to name 'attitudes' as evaluative placings on an attitude object. They can be measured. They exist.

It is also clear that these attitudes are somehow connected with 'beliefs' about an attitude object, where by 'belief' is meant any statement of any kind which connects the attitude object with some other object, goal or value. All the attitude measuring instruments discussed proceed by asking the subject to check his agreement or disagreement with certain beliefs. There is clearly some relationship between these beliefs and the 'attitudes' or evaluations which they are used to measure, even if we are so far unable to specify the nature of this relationship.

We have seen that it is far from clear in traditional attitude theory how attitudes are related to behaviour or to choice, though I have claimed that expectancy-value theory can clarify and demonstrate a relationship. Before discussing this theory, it would be useful to distinguish more carefully the concept of 'behaviour'. If we look at measurements of behaviour in the psychological literature (for instance, in the studies reviewed by Wicker, 1971) we find that what is called behaviour could usefully be sub-divided into:

(a) Behavioural intentions, i.e. intentions to engage in certain behaviour at various specified or unspecified times in the future.
(b) Reports of past behaviour . . . either on single or on multiple occasions, either observed or self-reported.
(c) Observations of behaviour taken after the attitudinal measures, consisting either of single or of multiple responses.

We will see later that relationships of attitudes to behaviour can be much clarified if the multiple ways in which 'behaviour' is measured are allowed for.

We are left then with three concepts; attitudes, beliefs and behaviour. It is the relationship between the three which we hope will illuminate the processes of choice. It is the relationship between the three which expectancy-value theory can clarify, test and observe.

Behavioural decision theory

Perhaps the best known expectancy-value model is the subjective expected utility (SEU) model of behavioural decision theory (Edwards, 1954) which has been widely used by, among others, those attempting to model micro-economic processes. According to this theory, when a person has to make a choice, he will select that alternative to which he personally attached the highest 'subjective expected utilities'. That is the alternative which he personally, in his own subjective judgement, believes will bring him the advantages he most highly values.

Edwards has proposed methods of measuring the SEU or 'subjective expected utility' of any given choice alternative. He measured the subject's expectation that the choice of any given alternative would bring him a certain value. This is of course a probability value (choosing such and such an alternative will *probably* bring me such a good) and can be given a number on a probability scale. It is symbolized in Edwards' equation as SP_i: the subjective probability that the choice of a certain alternative will lead to outcome i. Edwards also proposed ways of measuring the subjective value or utility to the person making the choice, of outcome i (such and such an outcome would seem to me good/bad). This subjective value can also be given a numerical position on a scale and is symbolized in Edwards' equations as U_i, the subjective utility or outcome of alternative i. Edwards then proposed that the over-all subjective expected utility of any given choice can be assessed by calculating a summation of the probabilities of *all* relevant outcomes of any given choice combined with the values attached to those outcomes.

This can be stated in equation form as:

$$\text{SEU} = \sum_{i=1} SP_i U_i$$

This model of Edwards was developed quite outside attitude theory; but note what happens if it is transformed into the language of attitudes. The model deals with *beliefs* about the consequences of performing a given behaviour. The model takes measures of all relevant beliefs about 'the consequences of performing a given behaviour'. It measures the probability value with which each belief is held (how likely it is that this action will lead to this outcome? These are the SP_i of Edwards' equation). It also measures the extent to which the values each of these probabilities linked to the attitude object are perceived as good or bad. (How good or bad would do I think each of these outcomes? These are the U_i of Edwards' equation.) Edwards' SEU or 'subjective expected utility' of any given outcome, is in our language an 'attitude'. It is a placing on an evaluative dimension of one specific attitude object, *the consequence of an action.*

Edwards therefore in this model has given us a very precise theory of the relationships of beliefs (probabilities and their attached values) to attitudes (subjective expected utilities). He has also suggested a relationship of attitudes (or SEUs) to behaviour, in so far as he theorizes that a man will choose the outcome to which he attaches the highest SEU. In our terms that is equivalent to saying he will choose the outcome to which he has the highest attitude measure, of which he is most 'in favour', when all relevant beliefs are taken into consideration. (The attentive reader will remember that in attitude research there is evidence that Edwards' choice theory is not always true in that choice does not correlate with favourability of attitude.)

Edwards' model is termed here an 'expectancy-value' model because its underlying theory is that men will choose in accord with their expectancies and their values.

Edwards' theory arose outside psychology proper in the area of decision theory; but from the work of Tolman in the 'thirties similar theories have developed in academic social psychology. This particular tradition of research and theory is little covered in B3 which concentrates more on the cognitive consistency schools (which postulate some sort of inner 'drive' towards consistency, rather on the lines of the dissonance theorists discussed at pp. 67–8), and on the functional schools of attitude theorists who take many insights from psycho-analytic work. Neither cognitive consistency theory or functional theory are in fact of any great use to those who wish to understand and specify the determinants of choice, in that (as Reich and Adcock point out) they fail to specify variables sufficiently clearly for measurement purposes and have failed to develop a coherent theory of the relationship between attitudes and behaviour. At the end of their review Reich and Adcock conclude, discussing the theories they have covered. 'It is difficult to predict specific behaviour by knowing someone's values and attitudes. The relationship between these concepts and behaviour is tenuous' (p. 129).

However the school of psychological study of attitudes which I have called 'expectancy-value' school is not so despairing. A clear and testable theory of the relationship of underlying concepts such as beliefs and attitudes to behaviour and to choice has been proposed in this tradition. Rosenberg (1956) was perhaps the first to introduce an explicit expectancy-value model in the attitude area, but the fullest statement of such a theory has been found in the work of Fishbein over the last decade. Until 1975 this was recorded mainly in scattered articles in the psychology journals (though some of those articles were brought together in a book of readings, *Readings in Attitude Theory and Measurement*, Fishbein, 1967). However, the 1975 text *Belief, Attitude, Intention and Behaviour*, by Fishbein and Ajzen, gives a full account of the theory and its research evidence. In the next chapter I shall give a brief outline of the nature of this theory.

6
Fishbein's theory: an exposition

In this chapter I shall attempt to give a brief outline of Fishbein's theory, accessibly to the non-psychologist and the non-mathematical reader. From time to time in the following chapter I will refer to giving numerical values to certain concepts. A full understanding of how this is done will depend on going through an example of the application of the theory which will be given in the appendix. But for the moment, those unfamiliar with survey or attitude measurement techniques, it would probably be useful to point out that essentially this theory is applied through paper-and-pencil tests. People are asked themselves to put numbers to their assessments of probability, their intentions, their assessments of the 'goodness' or 'badness' of various outcomes. Careful instructions are given before any questionnaire is completed, but essentially people are asked to answer questions such as the following:

On the whole do you think the following statement true or false, likely or unlikely? Check your answer on a scale running from *very true*, through *quite true* to *only slightly true*. You can mark the middle position which shows you are neutral or inbetween, or you can check the statement to be slightly untrue, quite untrue or very untrue:

TRUE *Very Quite Slightly*   *Slightly Quite Very* UNTRUE

The Conservative Party is in favour of hospital pay-beds.

Respondents are asked to put a cross at the place which most nearly represents their own judgement. The scale is then given numerical values ranging from $+3$ (very true) through 0 (neutral) to -3 (very untrue). Similar scales ranging from $+3$ to -3 can be given to obtain people's own assessment of the firmness of their intentions, of the values they attach to goals etc. etc.

Those inexperienced with these techniques suspect them as crude, simplistic and invalid. However there is an enormous weight of research evidence that most of the population can handle scales of this kind and that the results obtained from them are reliable and valid. The rubrics used to introduce the scales have much research and validation behind them to show they are comprehensible and result in consistent and meaningful scaling. This book is not the place to go into the research background which gives confidence in the use of such scaling methods, but the interested or sceptical reader is applied to such classics of questionnaire design as Moser (Moser and Kalton, 1971) or Oppenheim (1966).

The following chapter has been carefully written to make it accessible to those without mathematical background. However it is suggested that those who have no experience in measurement techniques should first read carefully through the chapter, then go through the example in the subsequent chapter, and then return to the theory. Only through considering theory and application together will the essential quality of the theory, its falsifiability, be understood.

Further preliminaries

A few further preliminary remarks must be made before we start to look at the theory proper. This book is called *How do we choose?* and Fishbein's theory is essentially a theory of behaviour under volitional control. Obviously some behaviour (such as the digestive processes or drug addiction) are not completely under volitional control, but the role of aware choice in our behaviour is in fact a very large one. Even psychoanalysts will agree that it is very large indeed and recent psychological work (for instance Ryan, 1970) suggests that it is even larger than we have traditionally thought.

Because the theory limits itself to questions of choice and

decision, it is possible to separate out the concept of behavioural intention. Before any act in which I decide to engage, there is a fractional antedating decision to engage in this act. I decide to get up and answer the door, to go on sitting at my desk or whatever. It is this immediate antecedent to overt behaviour which is described in the language of the theory as 'behavioural intention'.

Behavioural intention can have various levels of specificity. I have a vague general intention to go out one evening this week, I may have a more precise intention to go to the pictures one evening this week, I may have a yet more precise intention to go to such-and-such a film with such-and-such a person one evening this week. The more precise the behavioural intention which is measured the more likely it is to be accurately related to subsequent behaviour. Behavioural intention can of course change over time. I may have decided to go to the pictures but meet a friend on the way and 'change my mind'. Hence the more closely in time to the actual behaviour that behavioural intention is measured, the more accurately it will predict behaviour. The reason it is important to labour this concept of 'behavioural intention' is that normally, in our paper and pencil tests, we can only assess 'behavioural intention'. Respondents can tell us what they intend to do. And it is this behavioural intention which, in any given survey situation, must be the criterion variable to which we attempt to relate beliefs and attitudes. Once the concept of behavioural intention has been separated out, it becomes the task of the theorist to understand the roots of this behavioural intention. How is it formed? Can we predict it? Naturally we must also devise such measures of behavioural intention as are likely to relate to subsequent behaviour, and we must later check whether the measures of intention we have taken are in fact accurately predictive of subsequent behaviour. But our conceptual problem is to understand the relationship of beliefs to attitudes, of attitudes to behavioural intentions and of behavioural intentions to subsequent behaviour.

Origins of the theory

It was to this conceptual problem that Fishbein addressed himself. He was much influenced by the work of Dulany, an experimental psychologist in the learning theory area. Dulany had been working in the field of verbal conditioning, and he developed a theory, supported by much experimental work, of 'propositional control' (see Dixon and Horton, 1968).

The work in verbal behaviour will be unfamiliar to non-psychologists, but it is necessary to understand a little of what Dulany was doing to understand how his theory arose. At the time some psychologists argued that people could be 'conditioned without awareness'; that they could learn to engage in specific forms of verbal behaviour e.g. using first persons pronouns more often when the experimenter showed great interest and exclaimed 'aha' when they did so. Their behaviour was thought to be controlled by reinforcement mechanisms (see A3) and not necessarily volitional. The thrust of Dulany's work was to show that people in verbal conditioning experiments had a very good idea of what the experimenters were trying to do, and that their actions were, in fact, under the control of what they personally thought would be the rewards or otherwise of their actions, what they thought would be the value of these rewards or punishments, and (not least importantly) what they thought they were expected to do. In a series of experiments, Dulany showed that by working with this sort of cognitive variable, by taking into account people's own judgements, what people thought, he could predict very exactly what their intentions would be, and that their intentions also correlate very closely indeed with their actual overt behaviour.

Fishbein built on these insights, developed in the area of learning theory, to propose his own analysis of the factors underlying behavioural intention and choice.

A common-sense statement

Essentially, Fishbein argued that behavioural intentions are a function of two things; of a person's *attitude* to the behaviour in question, and a person's *subjective norm* about the behaviour in question. An example might make this more clear. Suppose I have a particular behavioural intention to get married tomorrow. The theory is saying that this intention is under the control of two other variables and two only. One is my *attitude* to the act of getting married tomorrow (and attitude is understood in the narrow Thurstone sense in which attitude has

77

always been measured: Do I think 'getting married tomorrow' would be nice or nasty, good or bad, beneficial or harmful? What is the number I would give it on some positive or negative scale of feeling?). The other is my subjective norm about getting married tomorrow (where normative belief is also understood in a narrow and specific sense: Do I believe that most people important to me think I should or should not 'get married tomorrow'?).

The theory is aiming at complete generality. 'Getting married tomorrow' is a purely arbitrary example. Any other act whatsoever could be substituted as an example, so long as it is an act preceded by a behavioural intention. It could be 'putting a new sheet of paper in the typewriter', 'getting up to have a cup of coffee', 'moving house', 'murdering my wife' or any other act at all about which it is possible to form an intention.

The disappointed reader may say at this point: 'But this so-called theory is only restating common sense. Of course my decision to do or not do something is dependent on whether I like or dislike the idea of doing it, and whether I think other people important to me think I should do it or not. This is merely elaborating on the obvious.' In a sense this is true; but it can be considered one of the strengths of the theory that the variables it suggests are intuitively acceptable to commonsense. The usefulness of formally specifying them may not be immediately obvious, but will soon be seen. The identification of these two and only two variables (the attitudal variable and the subjective norm) opens the way to formal measurement and testing procedures.

A formal presentation

I am aware that many readers of this book will be unsympathetic to or unfamiliar with the practice of reducing theory to formal mathematical expression, and may be tempted to skip equations such as those that follow hoping that their general meaning will rub off on them without attempting to follow measurement method. But it is essential to the kind of enterprise that psychologists and consumer behaviour theorists are engaged on, that general theory should be reduced to purely mathematical statements. Because it is only when theory is put in mathematical and measurable form, and precise methods of measurement are specified, that this theory becomes testable and hence falsifiable. In Chapter 1 various consumer behaviour theories were criticized because they were insufficiently precise and hence not open to falsification. The same criticism has been made of psychoanalytic models. It is important to understand the formal statements of Fichbein's theory, if the reader is to be convinced that the theory is specific, falsifiable and meaningful.

The theory is formally presented as an equation:

$$BI = Aact_{w1} + SN_{w2}$$

For the reader familiar with formal theories, it is sufficient to say that the proposed equation is a regression equation and that,

$$
\begin{array}{rl}
BI = & \text{behavioural intention} \\
Aact = & \text{attitude to the act} \\
SN = & \text{subjective norm} \\
w1 \text{ and } w2 = & \text{the regression weights of the equation to} \\
& \text{be empirically arrived at.}
\end{array}
$$

and

A reader to whom the meaning of the above is transparently obvious can skip the next two paragraphs. But other readers will need slightly more explanation. I beg them not to give up but to read the next two paragraphs carefully.

When a regression equation is being proposed, all that is being said is that it is known that two measurements we have, will together help us to predict the third measurement we want to have; but it is not known which of the two original measurements should be given the greatest weight in predicting the final measurement. Suppose we are considering a classful of school children. We know their marks in mathematics, we know their marks in French; but we don't know, though we wish to, their overall position in class. Both the marks in French and Maths will help us to predict their overall position in class. We'll make a *better* prediction of their overall marks in class by using both French marks and Maths marks than by either alone. But we don't know which set of marks, the French or the Maths, is closest to the final overall positions. We don't know which would be better at predicting the final overall positions in class. There are mathematical techniques by which we can find out: essentially by graphing all sets of marks and seeing which 'line' on the graph . . . the Maths line, or the French line is nearer, overall, to the final class position score we wish to predict. Once this has been done we can give a 'weight' to the Maths score and a 'weight' to the French score. These weights must be 'empirically arrived at', that is we can only calculate them if we have all the French scores, all the Maths scores, and all the final class position scores. But once they *are* empirically arrived at, we know the best way to combine the French and Maths scores to arrive at a prediction of the overall score for any individual child.

So to return to the Fishbein equation; what is being said is that the 'attitude' score (Do I like this act, approve of it or disapprove of it?) combines with the 'subjective norm' scores (Do I perceive of other people as thinking I should do it or shouldn't do it?) to form the behavioural intention score (Do I actually intend to do this act or not?) in some 'weighting' which can vary from groups of individuals to other groups, from situations to other situations . . . and that the 'weighting' given to attitude or norms can only be arrived at by a *post hoc* calculation against decisions. But the method for this *post hoc* calculation is rigorously specified according to normal mathematical procedures.

The regression equation proposed is, in fact, a powerful tool. It can tell us, about any given set of behavioural intentions, whether this set of behavioural intentions co-varies most with 'attitudes' (my liking or disliking for the act) or with 'norms' (by perception of what other people think I should do). For instance, if one had a measured set of behavioural intentions *vis-à-vis* reporting a traffic accident to the police, and also a measured set of attitudes *vis-à-vis* reporting the traffic accident, and a measured set of subjective norms, one could calculate whether the activity of reporting traffic accidents to the police tended to co-vary most with attitudes or with subjective norms.

Note immediately the importance of these concepts and measurements for the attitude-behaviour relationship. The regression equation is suggesting that yes, attitudes do sometimes affect behaviour. But they sometimes might have a low weighting in affecting behaviour. Certain behaviours may be influenced not so much by attitudes as by subjective norms. People may have a set of very negative attitudes about the reporting of traffic accidents to the police; this could be an act which they dislike, think unpleasant. Yet they may none the less do it, if this act turns out to be one which is heavily under the influence of subjective norms. They think they should report the traffic accident, this is what other people with power or other people important to them think they should do. So this is what they do, despite their negative attitudes.

The basic equation enables us, over any set of behaviours or set of people, to calculate weights for the extent to which this behaviour relates to subject attitudes or to norms. Is the kind of behaviour being measured here related to whether people *like* the consequences of the act or not (their 'attitude' or 'A act') or to whether they perceive other people as thinking they should engage in the act (their 'normative belief' or 'NB')?

Emphasis on attitude to act

Before leaving the basic equation, it is necessary to stress that the 'attitude' it proposed measuring is a very specific attitude, an attitude to a behaviour, to a possible choice we might make. Fishbein lays great stress on the fact that if we wish to predict or understand behavioural intention we must measure 'attitude to the behaviour', not attitude to the *object of* the behaviour. The point may appear unimportant but it has far reaching implications, and in itself helps to clarify the attitude-behaviour relationship. Researchers wishing to understand the roots of decisions to leave school, have traditionally looked at attitudes to 'school' and found little or no relationship with the act of 'leaving school'. According to Fishbein's theory they should be looking at attitudes to 'leaving school' which may well be totally different to attitudes to school. In the past studies of work relationships with immigrants, have attempted to relate actual behaviour *vis-à-vis* immigrants to overall attitudes to immigrants. According to the theory propounded here, it is not attitudes to immigrants which should be looked at, but attitudes to specific behavioural acts concerned with immigrants in the work situation.

We have seen that the basic equation

$$BI = Aact_{w1} + SN_{w2}$$

allows us to calculate weights for any given set of behavioural intentions, so that we can make some assessment of the relative contributions of the normative or attitudinal variable. But its usefulness and theoretic power go much further than this. Fishbein has proposed detailed theories of the origin and structure of both attitudinal and normative variables. These theories enable us to 'unpack' for any given individual, or set of individuals, the way in which the relevant attitudes affecting behavioural intention were formed from underlying beliefs; and the way in which the relevant subjective norm affecting behavioural intention was formed from underlying normative perceptions.

Let us first consider the structure and roots of the attitudinal variable. Here again Fishbein has proposed an equation:

$$Aact = \sum_{n}^{i} B_i e_i$$

Once more we will unpack this equation in detail in the next two paragraphs for the non-mathematical reader, but for the mathematical reader it should suffice to say that in the above equation

$Aact$ = Attitude to the act
B_i = Belief about the act; that is the probability that the act is related to some other object x_i
e_i = the evaluative aspect of B_i, that is the respondent attitude towards x_i
n = the number of beliefs.
Σ, of course, is the usual symbol for a sum over a set.

What exactly is being said? Fishbein is suggesting that for every act in which a subject might engage he has a set of beliefs about his act. These beliefs are simply any statement, insight or perception which links the act with some other value, object or goal. For instance, if the act is 'getting up from my typewriter for a cup of coffee' I currently have the beliefs:

'getting up for a cup of coffee would interrupt my train of thought'

82

'getting up for a cup of coffee would mean I could stretch
   and have a rest'
'getting up for a cup of coffee would waste valuable time'
   etc. etc.

For any given act which it is possible for me to conceptualize,
I will have at any given moment some such set of beliefs
linking the act with various other objects, goals or values. The
reader might care to pause at this moment and propose to
himself some possible future act and list briefly the first
'beliefs' or associations about such an act which come to
mind. Any act it is possible to conceptualize, any intention it
is possible to form, will have some 'beliefs' about consequences
or associations attached to it. Now it is the degree of probability with which these beliefs are held which is symbolized in the
equation above as B_i. B_i is the strength with which I believe
any one belief about the consequences of an act. e_i has been
defined above as 'the evaluative aspect of B_i. Any belief, such
as 'getting up for a cup of coffee would interrupt my train of
thought', links the act under consideration with another
concept towards which it is possible to have an attitude,
another concept which one evaluates. I have my personal
'evaluation' of 'interrupting my train of thought', and it is
an evaluation it is possible to measure and to give a number to
by usual attitude measurement procedures. Any belief at all
about anything will link the original object with some concept
goal or value which itself has some sort of evaluative weight.
I may rate 'stretching and having a rest' as a high positive,
and 'interrupting my train of thought' as a high negative.
Different people may have similar beliefs about the act of
'getting up for a cup of coffee' but may give them quite different evaluative weights. They may dislike 'stretching' and score
it negative but like 'interrupting my train of thought'. They
will, according to the equation, have a different *attitude*. I
myself will give different evaluative weights to my beliefs on
different occasions and hence come up with different attitudes
to 'getting up for a cup of coffee' on different occasions.

We are now able to put the proposed equation into ordinary
language. The formula

$$Aact = \Sigma B_i e_i$$

is saying that my overall attitude to any act (my feeling of
liking or dislike for it) is dependent on a certain set of beliefs or

Key

cognitions I have about this act. And it is dependent in a quite precise way. For any cognition I hold it is possible to measure how strongly I hold it; do I think it very true or doubtful, or even false? A number can be put on my probability judgement and this number is the B_i. For every belief I hold it is also possible to measure the 'evaluative aspect'. Do I think the concept, goal or value with which the belief links the original act, is good or bad, nice or nasty? A number can be put on this judgement and the number is the e_i. The equation is suggesting that if for each single belief I *multiply* the probability strength by the evaluative aspect (multiply B_i by e_i), and if I then sum the resultant product of these multiplications over the set of beliefs I hold about the act under consideration, the resultant number I come up with, the $\Sigma B_i e_i$ will be an equivalent number to a measurement of my overall attitude to the original act (*Aact*).

Discussion

In a sense this equation is only restating the insight that originally lay behind the attitude measurement systems of Likert, Thurstone and others. It is saying that overall attitude (or feelings of liking or disliking) are resultants of beliefs about the attitude object, of the strength with which these beliefs are held, and of the values with which they link the attitude object. But because this insight is formalized as an equation and precise measurement methods are suggested, it is formally testable. Testing is implicit in any application of the proposed measurement method. A set of beliefs about a given act is identified, then measured both for belief strength (B_i) and evaluative aspect (e_i) (more detail of the specific scales used will be given in the appendix to this chapter). The $\Sigma B_i e_i$ calculation is then carried out. Overall attitudes to the act are at the same time measured by any reliable measurement instrument which has previously been shown to be a valid measurement of attitude (see pp. 69–71). This *Aact* measure is taken independently of the B_i and e_i measures. For the mathematical reader it will be sufficient to say, that if the equation is not false, then *Aact* measures and $\Sigma B_i e_i$ measures must correlate; and in test after test they so do at a highly significant level, usually 0·6 or over.

The non-mathematical reader probably needs a word or two about the correlation statistic. Correlation statistics have been devised in order to measure the extent to which two sets of measures co-vary. To go back to our example of children's examination scores. It is probable that there is some degree of relationship between scores on Maths and French tests. Really clever children will do well at both, academically incapable children badly at both. The correlation statistic is a way of measuring how close this relationship is. It can vary from +1 to −1. A correlation of +1 means that the two sets of figures co-vary exactly. The order of the children in class for Maths and French is identical, and the spaces between the marks of first and second, second and third etc. are similar. (Note the two sets of marks need not have been made on the same scale. The French teacher may have marked out of 50, the Maths teacher out of 100, and still a perfect +1 covariance or correlation could occur.) A correlation of 0 means that there is no relationship whatsoever between the two sets of figures. Performance in Maths is totally unrelated to performance in French. A correlation of −1 means that there is a perfect *inverse* relationship between the two sets of figures. The child who is top at Maths will be bottom at French; and so on through the whole class with the child bottom at Maths coming top at French, and both order and distance between scores being equivalent but upside down throughout all the children.

The point to grasp is that the correlation statistic varies from +1 to −1 (and can pass through any decimal point between). +1 means exactly equivalent measures (though possible on a different scale), 0 means no relationship, and −1 means an inverse relationship.

If two different measures are taken *of the same thing* one expects perfect correlation. If height is measured for a whole class, first by metric and then in feet and inches, one would expect perfect correlations because both measurements are measuring the same dimension: height. Note it is possible for two measurements to correlate very significantly or very highly and *not* be measurements of the same underlying dimension (measurements of height and weight in normal school children are usually very highly correlated indeed). Correlation does not prove that the same underlying dimension is being measured. But if two measures are claimed to measure the same thing, they must correlate highly . . . or else it is clear that different entities are being measured.

To return then to the attitude equation, it can be tested (over a sample of people) by seeing if the two measures $Aact$ (measured on any reliable non-Fishbein scale, see p. 69) and $\Sigma B_i e_i$ (measured according to Fishbein's procedures, correlate highly. The $Aact$ and $B_i e_i$ measures have great surface dissimilarity. There is no obvious reason the measures should co-vary. These tests have frequently been carried out in the psychological literature, and so far, the equation seems to hold.

The usefulness of the equation

What follows if it holds? We can have confidence that the $\Sigma B_i e_i$ measures are measuring the same entity as 'attitude' defined as at p. 69. But what is more, the equation helps us to understand the relationship of given beliefs, the strengths with which they are held and the evaluations they carry with them, to overall feeling of dislike or liking. We can 'unpack' an attitude statistic, and relate it quite formally and precisely to underlying beliefs. I will know of a certain sample, not only that on the whole they 'like' or 'dislike' going to the pictures, but precisely what attributes of going to the pictures have combined in what way to set up this like or dislike. Relevance for consumer behaviour theory should already be clear. We can work out not only whether the consumer's act of, say, 'buying Oxo' depends more on 'attitudes' to buying or 'subjective norms' about buying (pp. 77–8) above; but also what beliefs a positive or negative attitude stems from, how strongly they are held, how good or bad the evaluations with which they link the act of 'buying Oxo'.

The subjective norm component

The theory not only proposes a way in which the attitudinal variable can be 'unpacked'; it does the same for the subjective norm variable. Work in the subjective norm area is more tentative, and less well-established, but there seems reason to believe that

$$NB = \Sigma SNB : Mc.$$

NB = generalized normative belief

SNB = measured belief strengths of social normative beliefs

Mc = motivation to comply with the referent

By 'social' normative beliefs are meant beliefs about what *other people* expect one to do. A set of relevant other people reidentified. For instance, for 'going to the pictures' they might be, my mother, my girlfriend, my boyfriend, my employer, people I meet at parties. The 'social normative belief' measures measure how strongly it is believed that each one of these relevant others might think I should go to the pictures. The equation proposes that my overall subjective norm (i.e. how strongly do I personally feel I should or should not go to the pictures) is related to the sum of these social normative beliefs.

Once again, the empirical evidence for this theory lies in the social psychological literature, and will not be recapitulated here. It is not as strong as the evidence for the $Aact = \Sigma B_i e_i$ equation. Indeed it has been impossible to demonstrate the role of the Mc or motivation to comply measures in the equation, and an alternative formulation:

$$NB = \Sigma SNB$$

(i.e. the single, overall, generalized normative belief correlates with measures over a set of individual social norms) seems to be more acceptable than the originally proposed equation

$$NB = \Sigma SNB : Mc$$

The concept of salience

So far in this discussion we have simply stated that 'a set of beliefs' about the concept, goals or values associated with an act, combine in the $\Sigma B_i e_i$ formula to produce attitude towards that act. It is worth pausing a little over what this 'set of beliefs' may consist of. Obviously about any given act there are an infinity of possible beliefs. Not all can be measured and identified. The theory does not propose that they should be. It states that the beliefs which combine to form attitude are those which are 'salient' at the time the attitude is considered for any given person. 'Salience' is given a precise operational definition. Salient beliefs are the first beliefs which a respondent produces in answer to an open-ended question such as 'Tell me what you think about (the act in question)'. The respondent is thought of as being his own best reporter on what beliefs are salient for him. Note he is not asked what beliefs are *important* to him, or what beliefs he *ought* to take into account in a given decision. He is simply asked to list the first beliefs and associations that come to mind about a given act, in a 'top-of-the-head' unconsidered way. There is considerable empirical evidence (Kaplan and Fishbein, 1969; Thomas and Tuck, 1975) that it is the first seven or so beliefs produced in answer to such an open-ended question which are really influential in forming attitude. Long ago (1956) George Miller argued in his essay 'The Magic Number seven plus or minus two' that for information handling reasons, the human brain seems only able to handle seven or so concepts at once at any given time. The theory is saying that it is these seven or so concepts which are uppermost at any one time which form attitude at any one time. Shifts in salience can, of course, occur. My salient beliefs about 'throwing the ship's cargo overboard' may be very different when my ship is quietly in dock, from when it is in a fierce mid-Atlantic storm. But then attitudes, too, will differ in different situations, and shifts in salience may well prove to be one of the major causes of attitude-change. The concept of 'shift in salience' as a major cause of attitude change is similar to a concept found recently in mass media research. Blumler (Blumler and McQuail, 1968) has argued that 'agenda setting' (control of topics seen as relevant) is the major way the media affect attitudes. 'Agenda setting' can be seen as a manipulation of belief salience.

Two and only two variables

We have now outlined the basic structure of Fishbein's theory in however over-simplified a way. One problem should perhaps immediately be taken up. A common objection to the theory is the paucity of the variables it considers. After all, it is saying that essentially behavioural intentions are controlled by only two things: attitudes or feelings of subjective liking or disliking and subjective norms. Again and again theorists wish to consider other variables. 'Situational' variables, 'demographic' variables, 'personality' variables. They feel that it is not enough to look only at the variables proposed by the theory. The equation is not saying that personality, situation, demographics have nothing to do with behavioural intentions. It is only saying that their effect on behavioural intentions is mediated through the two main variables of the theory, attitudes and subjective norm.

Clearly social class and age will come into the question of what values I associate with say, buying a Rolls-Royce. If I am rich and middle-aged, I may well believe that 'Buying a Rolls-Royce will bring me prestige', 'Buying a Rolls-Royce is something I can afford', 'Buying a Rolls-Royce will give me a reliable car . . . will give me a powerful car'. Some of these beliefs will be the same if I am young and poor, some of the evaluations may well be the same. But some will be importantly different. The young and poor will not believe 'Buying a Rolls-Royce is something I can afford'; will perhaps not believe that it would 'bring them prestige'; they may not evaluate prestige highly. The possible variations in the set of beliefs held, the strengths with which these beliefs are held, and their evaluations, are very large; the theory is saying that it is through these variations that variables such as 'demographics' (class and age status), 'personality', etc., are mediated. There is no need to measure them separately. Indeed the theory as it stands at the moment, says that no other variable has yet been identified which can help to explain more of the variance in decision than attitudes and subjective norms alone. Maybe some will be identified in the future. This is an empirical question. But so far, the proposal is that these two variables alone can account for all the variance in behavioural intention.

Levels of specificity

A further problem area to which attention is drawn by Fishbein is the necessity of giving thought to the 'level of specificity' on which one is operating. The theory is intended to be able to deal with any behavioural intention. But, as we pointed out at the beginning of this chapter, there can be many levels of specificity of intention. A general intention could be 'I intend

89

to go for a walk', but a more specific level of this intention is considered if the content, time and target of behaviour are fully specified. For example, 'I intend to go out for a walk on Hampstead Heath tomorrow afternoon with my dog'. Fishbein's theory can deal with both sorts of intention; but *only if all subsidiary measures are taken at precisely the same level of specificity as the behaviour it is wished to predict*. This is extremely important in application of the theory and can often be overlooked. (As a matter of fact it is extremely important in any applied social or consumer research, and is, I would claim, nearly always overlooked!) It is no good looking at attitudes to 'going for a walk' and subjective norms about going for a walk, and expecting them to predict precisely the behaviour of 'going for a walk tomorrow afternoon with my dog on Hampstead Heath'. The point is of particular importance for marketing. Overall attitudes to 'beer' will not necessarily have any relationship to the behaviour of 'ordering a Double Diamond in the pub on the corner when I go out for a drink tonight'.

Conclusion

A last point must be made before I leave this first statement of Fishbein's theory. It is intended as a model for *all* choice. I have sometimes found that when talking to marketing men about the model they will say:

> Oh yes. I can believe that Fishbein's theory might work splendidly for the large important kind of decisions that people look at in psychological work. It would probably work for decisions like would I live next door to an immigrant or something. But in marketing we're engaged in studying trivial, thoughtless kinds of decisions, like will I buy Andrex or Delsey or an own brand toilet paper. It wouldn't work for things like that.

Similarly I have found when talking to psychologists they have said:

> Oh yes. I can see why marketing men are working with Fishbein's theory. It probably works splendidly for trivial decisions like what kind of toilet paper people will buy. But

people couldn't possibly be making up their minds about really important questions affecting their whole lives by the kind of process you describe.

Alternatively I am told Fishbein's theory probably works for stupid people. They probably make up their minds in such a simplistic way; but it couldn't possible work for the intelligent. Or that it might make sense as a description of the thought processes of intellectuals, but no-one with a low IQ could possibly be operating in the way Fishbein suggests. Now, some or all of these remarks may be correct. The only tests are empirical. We must try out the theory and see. But I want to make clear that Fishbein's theory is *claiming* generality. It is a theory of all choice. It is a theory which can be disproved on any application. If it were found not to hold for some sub-group of acts or populations, it would need rethinking. So far, in my own wide research experience, and in the published studies, it has been found to hold.

Appendix to Chapter 6: an application of Fishbein's theory

The preceding chapter has laid out the essentials of Fishbein's theory in a simple form. But readers are probably left with questions as to the exact nature of the measures used. In this chapter, an example of an application of the theory will be given in order to demonstrate the kind of measurement technique used. However, a word of caution is necessary. Fishbein's theory is a theory; not a closed set of techniques. Once the theory is understood and absorbed, any practising researcher will find himself or herself coming up with slightly different research designs for any given problem. Published work with the theory has employed a multitude of different designs (for an overview of the work see Fishbein and Ajzen, 1975). The function of the following example is to help the reader to understand the *kind* of measurement technique and calculation which has been used to apply and test the theory.

The origin of the following example was a real-life study designed to shed light on the problem of wastage rates of recruits to the Women's Royal Army Corps. There are many more applicants for the British Women's Royal Army Corps than can possibly be accepted, and selection procedures are thorough, testing and careful. Despite this a certain number of applicants (quite small but appreciable; usually about 16 per cent) leave the Royal Army Corps after the first six weeks of basic training. This is clearly expensive and wasteful. The Army Personnel Establishment had examined sociological variables and cognitive scores for all entrants on preliminary screening, to see if they could find any way of discriminating between 'leavers' and 'non-leavers', but had been unable to find any differences. It was decided to see if a study of beliefs and attitudes could shed any light on the problem and show any differences between the beliefs or norms of those who left and those who stayed. The work was carried out by Kate Keenan, then of the Army Personnel Research Establishment (Keenan, 1976). The study was carried out in two stages.

Stage I was aimed at establishing a set of 'modal salient beliefs' about the act it was desired to study. At page 87 above it was argued that it is 'salient beliefs' that form an attitude and that 'salient beliefs' are those which a respondent produces in answer to an open-ended question, such as 'Tell me what you think about the act in question'. Now, clearly, every single individual may have a different set of salient beliefs about any given act. But for survey research purposes we cannot easily deal with a set of widely differing individual salient beliefs. Hence it is usually necessary to see if there is a set of 'modal salient beliefs', i.e. salient beliefs common to all likely respondents. This is done by administering and analysing an 'elicitation questionnaire' to a population similar in structure to the population on which the research proper is to be carried out. In this case, Keenan was interested to discover if 'salient beliefs' immediately on joining the army were different from or the same as those a few weeks later. She therefore elicited salient beliefs from two populations: firstly, 100 women within their first three days of joining the Army and, secondly, 100 women within the last few days of their initial six weeks of training. At each interview respondents were given a very simple basic questionnaire. It ran:

1. Can you tell me what you think about joining the WRAC? Just any ideas or views you have about joining the WRAC?
2. What do you think about making the WRAC your career?
3. Do you know anyone who thought you should join the WRAC?
4. Do you know anyone who thought you should not?

Some explanation of the above questionnaire is needed. I have stressed in the preceding chapter that beliefs, attitudes etc. should be measured on precisely the same level of specificity as the behaviour one wishes to predict. Why, then, did the questionnaire ask about 'joining the WRAC' and 'making the WRAC your career' when the action it was wished to predict was 'leaving the WRAC'? The reason shows the hazards of applied research. It was held by the sponsors of the research (the Womens' Royal Army Corps) that it would not be right to ask girls who had just within the last one to three days joined the Army to consider 'leaving the Army'. They were not willing to allow the question 'what do you think about leaving the Army?' to be posed to these girls. Keenan judged after some pilot work that the actions of 'leaving the Army' or 'joining the Army' were in fact semantically and meaningfully very close to each other within the first six weeks of entrance. She therefore decided to specify the act in which she was interested as 'joining the army' or 'not joining the Army' and to concentrate all her measurements on this act. However, at the elicitation stage, she was not entirely confident that this would be the best wording, so the second concept 'making the WRAC your career' was included to see if this elicited a different set of salient beliefs, or if the set of salient beliefs it elicited showed any differential shift over time to the set elicited from the first question. Keenan's procedure here is a good example of how a researcher cannot always proceed by rule of thumb, but must work from a genuine understanding of underlying theory. The essentials are to elicit beliefs about the act to which one is later going to measure attitudes and monitor behaviour, and to elicit on the same level of specificity throughout any study.

Questions 3 and 4 on the elicitation questionnaire were included to discover what other people were perceived by the girls to be relevant to their decisions. This information is needed to prepare 'social normative belief' questions for Stage II of the study.

A careful content analysis of the elicitation questionnaire was carried out and replies to each question tabulated for frequency of occurrence. As expected, certain responses occurred in all samples with markedly greater frequency than others. It also became clear that Question 2 did produce beliefs different in kind from those to Question 1. Keenan prepared the following list of beliefs which accounted for 65 per cent of all responses at Time 1 (within three days of joining) and 90 per cent of all elicited beliefs at Time 2 (within the last three days of the six weeks training period).

Joining the WRAC: gives me opportunities to travel
means mixing with different people, making new friends
is a chance to get a career, learn a trade, offers me better career prospects than exist at home
could mean promotion for me
gives me independence
means good pay
gives me security
gives discipline
means being away from home
means lots of restrictions (lights out, too many rules, etc.)
means having to get up at 6.30
means too much cleaning (uniform, rooms, etc.)

The elicitations showed no major difference between beliefs salient at Time 1 and Time 2; though most beliefs found to be modally salient at Time 1 had become *more* frequent and accounted for a greater proportion of all responses at Time 2. Experience (and this is not un-typical of similar studies) had led to a certain 'solidifying' or 'stereotyping' of beliefs.

It is worth mentioning here that if an elicitation study does *not* throw up a clearly dominant set of modal salient beliefs, then further studies must be carried out before continuing to Stage II. The usual cut-off point taken is that the beliefs selected for the final questionnaire must account for *at least* 60 per cent of all recorded responses. If this is not happening, the spread of 'individual salients' is so wide and idiosyncratic that the topic is not suited to survey research techniques without further breakdown into sub-samples with more similar salients. In research on the usage of any advertised product, salient beliefs are almost always more stereotyped than on research into non-advertised products. Usually 5 to 7 modal salient beliefs will account for 70 per cent of all recorded responses. Advertising in all probability works through controlling respondents salient beliefs about using a product.

Keenan's analysis of Questions 3 and 4 produced the following set of relevant others: my mother, my father, my relations, friends in the services, relatives in the services, people at work, my boyfriend.

Keenan analysed salient beliefs and salient relevant others to see if there was any marked difference in elicitation levels for those later (through their behaviour) found to be 'leavers' or 'stayers' in the WRAC. There were in fact some differences. For 'leavers' career responses were less frequently salient even at Time 1, and responses about the problems of discipline and excessive cleanliness were more frequently present.

Some consumer behaviour studies have been carried out which have used solely the Stage I elicitation technique just described to shed light on the differential beliefs underlying attitudes of 'users' or 'non-users' of a product. An example is recorded in the literature (Fallan and Tuck, 1973).

However, Keenan went on to construct a full quantified Stage II study from her elicitation results. The measures included in her questionnaire were as follows:

1. A measure of behavioural intention as regards the act it is intended to predict. The measure used was as follows: 'As far as you can judge at the moment, do you want to stay in the WRAC after your training at Guildford? (Remember your answers to this question are *entirely* private.)'

I want to stay in WRAC after my training at Guildford	AGREE				DISAGREE		
	Totally	Mostly	Some-what	Neutral or inbetween	Some-what	Mostly	Totally

2. A measure of over-all attitude to the act being predicted. The measures used were as follows: 'Now we want you to check your personal opinion about joining the WRAC.

'Would you say that "joining the WRAC" was a good or a bad thing for you *personally* to do?

GOOD	Totally	Mostly	Some-what	Neutral or inbetween	Some-what	Mostly	Totally	BAD

'Would you say it was foolish or wise?

	Totally	Mostly	Some-what	Neutral or inbetween	Some-what	Mostly	Totally	
FOOLISH								WISE

'Would you say it was beneficial or harmful?'

	Totally	Mostly	Some-what	Neutral or inbetween	Some-what	Mostly	Totally	
BENEFICIAL								HARMFUL

3. An overall measure of normative belief. The following is the exact wording used: 'On the whole would you say most of your friends and family approved or disapproved of you joining the WRAC?'

	AGREE				DISAGREE		
Most of my friends and family approved of my joining the WRAC	Totally	Mostly	Some-what	Neutral or inbetween	Some-what	Mostly	Totally

4. Measures of the belief strength with which modally salient beliefs identified at elicitation were held. Subjects were asked to tick whether they agreed totally, mostly or somewhat with each belief, were neutral or inbetween, or disagreed somewhat, mostly or totally. Practice items were gone through and then subjects completed the scales themselves. Beliefs were phrased as elicited, e.g. 'Joining the WRAC gives me opportunities to travel'.

5. Measures of the evaluative aspects of the modally salient beliefs identified at elicitation. Subjects were asked to check whether 'certain things connected with joining the WRAC seem to you *good* or *bad*. You can check from *Extremely good*, through *Quite good*, *Slightly good*, *Neutral or inbetween* to

Slightly bad, Quite bad, Extremely bad'. The items given to evaluate were the objects, goals or values with which the elicited modally salient beliefs had linked the attitude object 'joining the WRAC'. They included items such as 'discipline', 'getting up early', 'making new men friends', 'security', etc., etc., all phrased in the verbal form in which they had been most frequently elicited.

6. Measures of normative beliefs re relevant others found to be salient at elicitation. These took the following form:

> 'Now we want you to check whether people thought it was a good idea for you to join the WRAC. Don't forget you can always check the *Neutral or inbetween* space if you feel this question does not apply to you.'

Subjects were then given self-completion scales asking them to check from *Totally agree* through to *Totally disagree* for each of the normative others, e.g. 'My mother thought it a good idea I should join the WRAC' etc.

7. Measures of motivation to comply to each of same set of normative others. Here the wording went: 'Some people we like to fit in with; about others we couldn't care less. On the whole do you wish to fit in with or not fit in with what the following people might think you should do?' (Subjects asked to rate on usual type of 7-point scale.)

Analysis

Data was analysed in two stages. The first stage was to see if the measures taken fulfilled the predictions of Fishbein's theory cit. This analysis must always be carried out in work with Fishbein's theory. If it does not hold some basic error has been made or the theory has been falsified. The main Fishbein equation runs.

$$BI = Aact_{w1} + NB_{w2}$$

This means that a high multiple correlation of the *BI* measure (number 1 above) with the *Aact* and *NB* measures (numbers 2 and 3) should be found. Fishbein also suggests that *Aact* is a resultant of belief strengths (symbolized as B_is and measured at number 4 above) combined with evaluative aspects (symbolized as e_is and measured at number 5 above) and summed across the set of salient beliefs. The formula he presents is:

$$Aact = \Sigma B_i e_i$$

A high correlation between $Aact$ (measured at number 2 above) and $\Sigma B_i e_i$ (constructed from measures at numbers 4 and 5) should also be found. Fishbein has also suggested that NB (number 3 above) is a resultant of the detailed normative measures taken at 6 and 7 above. The exact way in which these measures combine to form NB is still a topic of research, but Fishbein's most recent proposal is that $NB = \Sigma SNB$, where SNB represents a summation of measures taken at number 6 above. We therefore expect a high correlation between NB and ΣSNB. It is necessary also to check if the paper and pencil BI measure in the questionnaire relates to observed real-life behaviour later. After the data was analysed to see if it supported Fishbeinian theory, it was looked at in detail to see what direct light it could throw on underlying reasons for leaving or staying in the WRAC.

Results – did they fit the model?
To sum up over-all, behavioural intentions were highly related to the actual concrete behaviour which followed. Behavioural intention correlated 0·68 with behaviour when measured at Time 1 (immediately after joining) and 0·86 with behaviour when measured at Time 2 (near the end of basic training).

The other predictors of the Fishbeinian equations showed high success in accounting for the variance in behavioural intention. The multiple correlation of $Aact$ and NB with behavioural intention was 0·59 at Time 1 and 0·73 at Time 2.

The correlations of the $\Sigma B_i e_i$ measure with $Aact$ were highly significant at Time 1 and Time 2 ($= 0·47$ Time 1, 0·61 Time 2). Similarly the correlations of ΣSNB with the global NB measure were highly significant ($R = 0·58$ Time 1, 0·56 Time 2).

The general pattern of these results gave Keenan confidence that she had been measuring beliefs which genuinely related to behavioural intention, that behavioural intention was genuinely related to behaviour, and that a substantial portion of individual girl's decisions could be understood from her data.

Results – practical interpretation
Keenan considered the results of the study as supportive of Fishbein's general theoretic position. But how were the results interpreted in detail? Could she use them to shed practical

light on women's reasons for leaving or staying in the army? Did they offer a real way of discriminating between future 'leavers' or 'stayers' at an early stage?

This question was answered by comparing the mean belief strength of all beliefs measured, of all evaluations measured, of all norms measured, and of all motivation to comply measured, to see if there were statistically significant differences between the way these measures were scored by 'leavers' or by 'stayers'. In fact there were.

The strength of beliefs that joining the army meant making new friends, good promotion prospects, too much cleaning, etc. did not in fact differ between those subsequently found to be stayers and those subsequently found to be leavers. It was as if their cognitive perception of the army was very similar. The only belief measurement difference which reached statistically significant levels was that the stayers believed more strongly that the army offered them good career prospects. There were, however, several important statistical differences on the evaluative side of the equation. The e measure showed that stayers felt very much more positive about making new friends, independence, discipline and being away from home than did leavers.

The attitudinal side of the equation was more closely related to behavioural intention and subsequent behaviour than was the normative. However, there was one normative difference which reached a significant level between leavers and stayers: stayers were more likely to have the support of their mother and father i.e. those whose mothers and fathers approved of them joining the Army were more likely to remain than those who left.

Usefulness of study

The study was in fact used to create a new instrument for measuring girls' beliefs and attitudes about 'joining the army' before they actually joined; and the validity of this new instrument in discriminating leavers from stayers is still being investigated. The study has also been used to offer informal guide-lines to those who interview applicants, who are instructed to lay stress on aspects of the service which 'leavers' find unattractive. Clearly it is in the interests of the Army not to attract recruits who will be lost to them.

The study also demonstrates one way in which Fishbein's

theory can be applied for commercial work. A study of almost identical type could be quite cheaply carried out on 'buying' or 'not buying' a product, with analyses made of the differences in strengths of beliefs and norms between buyers and non-buyers, Northerners or Southerners, old or young, etc.

7
Some further cognitive theories

The preceding chapter and its appendix have described one particular example of expectancy-value theory, Fishbein's theory. It has been made clear that Fishbein has not been working alone in this area. Rosenberg (1956) has proposed a similar model of attitudes, and the roots of expectancy-value theory can be traced to the work of Tolman (1932) and of Osgood (1957). Neither has Fishbein's theory remained unchallenged.

The main challenge to Fishbein's work has come from Jagelish Sheth, co-author of the Howard and Sheth book on consumer behaviour discussed in Chapter 2 (Tuncalp and Sheth, 1974; Sheth and Park, 1973). The argument between Sheth and Fishbein is complex, and any interested reader must go to the original sources to discover for himself where he feels the weight of proof lies. I shall try to clarify the issues.

The reader of Chapter 6 will remember that Fishbein's formula $Aact = \Sigma B_i e_i$, implies that only two dimensions of belief are relevant in the formulation of attitudes; the strength with which they are held to be true (the 'B' measure) and the evaluative direction of the belief, that is, whether it connects the original attitude object with value perceived as 'good' or 'bad' (the e measure). Sheth contended, with some plausibility, that this formula ignores any measure of the *importance* of beliefs. Some strongly held and evaluated beliefs may *not*, he would argue, affect attitude because they are 'unimportant' beliefs in the context of some particular judgement. For example, if one were attempting to investigate a man's attitude to the act of 'joining the Army' the beliefs 'Joining the Army would mean having to polish my shoes every day' and 'Joining the Army would mean, perhaps, being killed in Vietnam' would have the same weight in Fishbein's formula if both beliefs were in the salient set. Sheth would argue that these two beliefs, even though they were held equally strongly, are clearly not of the same *importance* or relevance to the given decision, and hence should not be given such equal weight.

One way proposed dealing with this problem has been to substitute for the Fishbein e, or evaluative measure, an i, or importance measure. Subjects have been asked to check on a scale the degree of importance they attached to different beliefs in deciding on a behaviour, and this 'degree of importance' was fed into the equation. Note that it is very different to ask a subject 'How important do you think having to polish your shoes every day is to your decision to join or not join the army?' from asking 'Is polishing your shoes every day something you think a good thing or a bad thing?' Very different scaling values will ensue from the two different questions.

In some so-called tests of Fishbein's theory in the research literature, the 'importance' measure described above was systematically substituted for Fishbein's evaluative measure, either through misunderstanding, or because the researcher genuinely thought the 'importance' scale was measuring the same thing.

However, Fishbein himself has consistently argued that the substitution of an importance measure for an evaluative measure in his equation is intellectually mistaken and results in poorer empirical correlations with attitude. Remember that the Fishbein equation is meant to apply only to *salient* beliefs (see p. 87 above) and that Fishbein proposed and used an operational definition of salience as the *first* seven beliefs a respondent produces in answer to an open-ended question such as 'tell me what you think about (the act or object in question)'. According to Fishbein it is through salience that any 'weighting for importance' enters the psychological process. If 'Joining the army would mean having to polish my shoes every day' is something that immediately occurs to a man when asked about 'joining the army', then it is salient for him, it *is* 'important' for him. The theory specifies that the seven or so beliefs that occur to a man at any given moment about the ends of his action are all 'important' for his attitude to that action; that they would not so occur to him if they were not 'important' or causative in deciding his attitude to that action.

This theory can on occasion seem counter-intuitive. If a researcher finds the two beliefs about 'joining the army' (it would mean polishing shoes daily; it would mean possibly being killed) equally salient, he is not really happy about allowing both equal weight in the prediction of attitude to 'joining the army'. He feels, as a sensible man, the latter *must* be more important than the former. So there is an intuitive plausibility to some attempt to modify Fishbein's formula by allowing in extra 'importance' weighting.

Essentially Sheth's own model neglects the 'salience' concept, but gives 'importance weights' to beliefs through *post hoc* regression techniques. He established a criterion measure, such as over-all attitude to a product or to buying a product, and calculates (by regression techniques; see p. 79) which of a given set of beliefs most accurately predicts this criterion measure. He transforms this into an 'importance weighting' and then feeds it back into an equation for predicting attitude. This of course involves circularity. If a mathematical calculation of what belief is most closely related to attitude in a given empirical situation is allowed into the formula for predicting attitude, naturally the formula so arrived at will perform pretty well as an attitude predictor.

Inevitably if one begins a research knowing the answer one wants and weights the initial variables one combines by their success in predicting this answer, one is likely to come up with more accurate results than if initial variables are combined in ignorance of the final answer. Sheth's model does the former: the answer is allowed to influence the calculation. Fishbein's the latter: the calculation stems from *a priori* principles. The closeness of the results of comparison, with rarely any statistical difference between the correlations found, argues, in my view, in favour of Fishbein's work.

A continuing argument

The issue still remains a contentious one. Undoubtedly at some point Fishbein's theory will be improved upon; but my reading of the current state of the research literature is that Sheth has so far failed to demonstrate any preferable method of procedure.

Other researchers using cognitive variables have been using still other approaches; two of which at least must be discussed since they have achieved considerable popularity. These are multi-dimensional scaling and trade-off analysis.

Multi-dimensional scaling

Multi-dimensional scaling is a mathematical technique, itself with no theoretical implications. However, its usage in consumer behaviour research has been associated with a particular theoretic position. Before this is discussed the nature of the technique itself must be indicated. (Those who wish to go further can find a useful introduction to the technique in Christopher, 1973.)

Context-free multi-dimensional scaling has been developed to assess the minimum number of dimensions it is necessary to postulate to explain a given set of difference judgements. That may seem a difficult sentence; but an example should make the principle clearer. Suppose an investigator wants to discover the relevant dimensions along which three objects A, B and C are compared. As a first step he could ask subjects to judge the degree of similarity between the three possible pairs of objects (AB, AC and BC) on a seven-point scale ranging from similar (0) to dissimilar (6). Suppose Subject 1 rates AB = 2, BC = 3 and AC = 5. Suppose Subject 2 rates AB = 3, AC = 4 and BC = 5. The analytic problem of the multi-dimensional scaler is to determine the number of dimensions necessary to locate objects A, B and C in space in accordance with their distance from each other. Subject 1 is easy. Only one dimension is necessary to account for his distance estimates:

$$AB = 2$$
$$BC = 3$$
$$AC = 5$$

Subject 2 is a little more complex; one dimension alone will not allow us to map his distance estimates accurately:

$$AB = 3$$
$$BC = 5$$
$$AC = 4$$

But if two dimensions are used it is possible to represent Subject 2's distance estimates accurately:

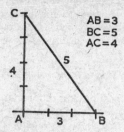

AB = 3
BC = 5
AC = 4

It is possible to analyse for any given set of difference judgements the number of dimensions required to map them accurately.

The attraction of this technique to theorists of choice behaviour is that it seems to offer the possibility of moving direct from a set of consumer preference judgements (suppose Subjects 1 and 2 above had been recording their perceptions of similarities and dissimilarities between different TV programmes A, B and C; or had been expressing their attitudes to different soap-powders A, B and C), to an assessment of how many dimensions the consumers are using to choose. Indeed, the technique will tell us how many dimensions are being used in the consumer's mental processes, if we can accept the assumption (which seems a not unreasonable one) that the more similar a pair of objects, the closer their location in multi-dimensional space. (There is of course an underlying assumption which might or might not be psychologically accurate that multi-dimensional space is a good 'model' or analogy for mental processes.) However the problem of the *naming* of the dimensions identified by a multi-dimensional analysis remains, and in applied research is usually solved in an intuitive or commonsense manner. Thus a researcher may establish that four dimensions are needed to map adequately consumer judgements of the differences or similarities between television programmes. He proceeds to 'name' these dimensions essentially by preparing maps using the four dimensions of all the programmes and observing from his knowledge of the programmes what seems to be causing the similarity groupings. He may decide there is a 'talk–music' dimension and a 'current affairs–entertainment' dimension . . . he will himself judge what *are* the dimensions which he has discovered.

This is the weak point of the technique. Because of its mathematical sophistication it can give an air of spurious certainty to what are in fact researcher judgements of the nature of the grounds of choice. The researcher argues that the dimensions his scaling has uncovered are the dimensions on which the consumer is basing his difference–similarity decisions and hence by naming them, he has told the client the nature of the dimensions influencing choice. For anyone employing multi-dimensional scaling as a research technique into the nature of choice, the crucial area of the study to pay attention to is the grounds on which the researcher has named his dimensions. In many applied studies in the consumer behaviour field, these grounds will be seen themselves to be logically inadequate. A particular dimension may be named as say 'Liberal–Conservative' with superficial plausibility. Further examination could show it might just as easily have been named 'Geographical origin of candidates'. One of the dimensions which emerge from a study of preference judgements will certainly be an over-all evaluative or attitudinal dimension (How much do the subjects like or approve of objects A, B and C?). This is often forgotten and the general evaluative dimension given some other and misleading name.

In sum, multi-dimensional scaling is not a theory of behaviour but a technique, and a technique of some usefulness. Students of choice behaviour should not however be misled into thinking it offers some theoretic framework alternative to others we have discussed.

Trade-off analysis

Trade-off analysis is nearer to offering a theory of consumer behaviour. The basic idea is that people make choices by 'trading-off' one valued attribute of a product or choice-alternative against another. Consumers are asked as the initial point of any trade-off study to play a matrix game about their choices. They may be asked for instance to decide what car they would buy if given a choice of cars with different combinations of colour, mileage per gallon and speed. Matrices are given to the consumer which allow him to make a great many choices between say a black car which will go very fast, and a black car which is slower; a red car which does forty miles to the gallon and a black car which does only twenty miles to the gallon, etc., etc. Through mathematical analyses it is possible to make a judgement as to which 'cue' provided seems to be influencing choices most. Is the consumer choosing mainly on colour and only secondarily on speed and economy; or is there some other order?

The dangers of the technique lie firstly in the artificial nature of the original games the subject is asked to play. The named dimensions given in the study may not be the right ones. Maybe in real life the consumer isn't choosing on colour, speed or economy at all but one size of car, or some other dimension the researcher has never thought to include in his study. Even if the right real-life dimensions are there, maybe the artificial matrix game the respondent is asked to play does not represent the way his mind moves in the real-life market. If Fishbein's theory is correct, different dimensions may well be salient to the consumer naturally than those made artificially salient by the game. There are further problems to do with the interpretation of the regression weights given to the cues (speed, economy and colour) in the mathematical analysis. It is of course possible to identify the cues which are the most accurate statistical predictors of the choice which ensues, and the different cues will then be arranged by the researcher in order of 'importance'. But 'importance' is a slippery word. And the best statistical predictor of final choice may not be the factor which, if changed or altered, actually influences final choice (see p. 44 above).

Those interested in trade-off analysis are referred to Westwood, Lunn and Beazley (1974), who lay out in lucid and accessible form the essentials of the technique and give references for further reading. In my own opinion the model, though interesting, makes too many assumptions which have not been validated to be trustworthy in application at its present stage. But it is an ingenious technique and one of which more will be heard.

Conclusion

This chapter has described some work critical of the Fishbein model in the expectancy-value area and indicated some recently popular techniques in multi-variate analysis. Some of the issues raised remain to be classified. Multi-dimensional scaling is a useful technique of which we will undoubtedly hear much more. The next decade should show whether the challenges to Fishbein's work succeed as we must hope they do, in improving on his model. For the moment no critic has succeeded in indicating preferable procedures for understanding the relationships of beliefs, attitudes, norms, intentions and behaviour; in a word, for understanding 'how we choose'.

Part Three
EXAMPLES AND APPLICATIONS

In Part One we surveyed the theories of consumer behaviour currently extant in both the academic consumer behaviour area and in the practical word of marketing men and researchers. We came to the conclusion that most of the models available are 'models without facts'; interesting mental exercises but essentially untestable. Some theorists argue that consumer behaviour is essentially stationary and that no choice model is necessary to understand it, since only the reinforcement of existing behaviour is relevant. It was argued that the 'reinforcement' versus 'conversion' argument which has bedevilled both consumer behaviour theory and theories of voting behaviour, is essentially irrelevant, in that both processes are essentially ones of becoming more rather than less likely to choose a given alternative.

In Part Two psychology, in particular attitude theory, was examined to see what it had to offer to those who wished to understand choice behaviour. It was suggested that attitude theory as developed until the late 'sixties had in fact little usable to offer in helping to predict or understand choice behaviour. Up until the late 'sixties, psychologists had done much useful work in clarifying the attitude concept and in demonstrating the measurability of attitudes, but they had been unable to produce a precise and testable theory of the relationship of attitudes to behaviour. In Chapter 6 it was suggested that the recent rise of expectancy-value theory, and in particular of Fishbein's very carefully specified version of this theory, offers students of choice behaviour a more ready means of understanding and research than has hitherto been available.

In Part Three we shall examine some actual examples of research into choice behaviour. A great deal of this research is of course in the area known as consumer behaviour. It is carried out by market research agencies and by marketing companies. It is designed to help manufacturers to sell. But many other people are researching choice; students of transport behaviour, students of occupational psychology, students of voting behaviour. In fact the kind of research which is wanted by policy makers in a democratic society is very often research into choice. Our governors wish to know why we go to the doctor, often or infrequently, why we prefer certain housing estates to others, why children smoke, what would persuade us to accept an incomes policy. Much applied research, though not conceptualized as research into choice behaviour, is, in fact, attempting to answer questions about choice; or perhaps it would be more accurate to say that the commissioners of the research would *like* it to answer questions about choice, though the academics who carry it out are unsufficiently convinced of any choice model to be able to supply any answer of that sort. I am convinced that much of the dissatisfaction of policy makers with social science research springs from this sort of mismatch.

Part Three will attempt both to survey briefly the kind of applied research currently being carried out, and to give detailed examples of particular researches which have been successful in answering choice questions. Particular attention will be given to those studies which have used the expectancy-value theory.

8
Consumer behaviour research now

The best indicator of 'where it's at' in consumer behaviour research, is the volume of research carried out commercially at any given time, by market research agencies and by consumer marketing companies. In Great Britain at the moment (1976) unquestionably the most popular and widely used method of research into consumer behaviour is the group discussion (see pp. 45–6 above).

The reasons are, of course, partly economic; a few group discussions can be carried out for a few hundred pounds, and in these times of financial stringency no-one wants to spend a lot of money.

But it is not quite so simple as that. The swing to small-scale research and the enormous emphasis put on 'groups' has other causes than sheer economy. I believe a large part of the cause is a disillusioned reaction from elaborate multivariate studies of the type discussed at page 42 above.

The 'sixties and the early 'seventies were the time of the computer. Researchers were excited by the way in which the computer allowed them to deal with calculations of a size and complexity hitherto impossible. No matter how many variables the researcher decided to measure, the computer could deal with them all and come up with neatly ordered tables. The usual procedure became to examine and measure a great many variables and to allow the computer to decide (mainly on regression criteria) which ones best predicted the dependent variables. For several reasons, some of which I discussed in

115

Chapter 2, the results of these applications of multivariate techniques were not always entirely happy. Clients discovered that they had bought an elaborate and expensive body of research, which either gave them results which they felt they knew all along, or which produced counter-intuitive results they were unable to trust. The measures of the basic variables which entered into the study were often difficult to comprehend or interpret, the listing at the end of the study of 'influential factors' in order of importance often seemed contrary to commonsense and intuition. And since the clients who bought the research rarely understood the basic mathematics, they were left with the option of either trusting the counter-intuitive results of some researchers whose techniques they did not understand, or of throwing the research away and trusting their own judgement. If the research did go along with their own preconceptions, they were equally disillusioned, because they tended to think 'Look, I have spent all these thousands of pounds to tell me something so obvious I knew it anyway.'

If, by any rare chance, counter-intuitive results were trusted and action taken as a result of them, it was rarely possible to show clearly that this was successful. This is a common problem in studies of advertising or marketing effectiveness. The variables of distribution, pricing, competition and advertising are too multitudinous to make clear assessment of effects easy. If action taken as a result of a research failed to show an increase in sales, the marketing man was strengthened in his distrust of the technique.

Meanwhile motivational research continued to be popular. Motivation research reports have the great advantage that clients feel they can understand them. There is no elaborate mathematics . . . you only have to be able to read. Also the results tend to have the splendid quality of being neither counter-intuitional nor banal. The client feels 'Oh I had never thought of that. But it does sound likely.'

To make clearer what I mean, let us consider some examples of the results of motivational research studies as quoted in an excellent recent review of this type of work (Mostyn, 1976). Mostyn lists the following examples of applications of motivational research, arrived at from consideration of discussion groups or depth interviews:

Examples of applications to product development
... Keep the sting in the antiseptics Mum uses on children's cuts so that she can supply the comfort.
... Large, tall, thin cereal packets appeal to Mums who like the cornucopia look when a small child pours from a pack as big as he is.
... Gardeners feel that digging the soil is part of the creative process; a new soil conditioner promising no digging had to modify its product so that the gardener had to do some of the most important initial digging (not the heaviest), so that the user could feel he had earned his garden through his own sweat.

Examples of applications to the design of ads
... Part of the appeal of smoking cigars for a man is that women dislike 'the old smelly things' – it is a man's chance to be a messy, dirty little boy again. Commercials showing a woman offering cigars around after dinner to the men, offended men.
... Sweets need to be advertised as either sources of energy or status symbols (*After Eights*) to compensate for the childish, self-indulgent and unhealthy associations in the consumer's mind.
... An airline in the States running a service to Australia showed a picture of someone digging a hole through the earth, featuring the slogan 'We know the shortest way round the earth'. This incited fears of planes crashing and making holes in the ground and images of burial grounds.'

The striking thing about all the above results is that they are the kind of conclusions that the average commercial client *likes*. They are not difficult to understand. They are actionable ... he knows what to do as a result of them. They make him feel knowing, but not too surprised. No wonder they are popular.

But there is one over-riding problem. Are they true? Perhaps indeed most mothers like antiseptic ointments to sting a little so they can comfort their children. But perhaps some mothers would prefer the ointments to soothe? How can we really know? The 'results' of the motivation research are in most cases simply clever insights; hypotheses which need thorough future testing before they can be trusted. Yet very rarely are they presented in this way.

117

Groups for all seasons

The continuing popularity of 'motivation research' and the declining popularity of mathematical, multivariate studies led to the application of the group discussion method for more and more purposes. In United Kingdom commercial research today, whether the aim be to check out the communicative meaning of a given advertisement, to test reactions to a new product, to discover past habits of buying, to discover house-wives' views about currently available products . . . almost whatever the purpose, the research method of choice will be discussion groups.

The problems of validity are rarely faced, much less solved. The occasional researcher (e.g. Twyman, 1973) will be curious enough to set up duplicate 'group discussions' with different discussant–reporters, to see if results are replicated. In the Twyman study referred to they were not. Each group discussant came up with a different conclusion, as indeed any student of group dynamics and selective perception would expect. Essentially most mass commercial activity in group discussions is not research at all. It is a comfort mechanism for decision makers. Its sociological function is to provide hypotheses or confirmations which spread the responsibility for action.

Ethnomethodology

It is not only in commercial research that there has been a retreat from the attempt to arrive at widely applicable and valid conclusion into small-scale and exploratory work. Sociology too has been experiencing a similar shift in fashion. Since Goffmann and Garfunkel it has been more and more the orthodoxy that researchers should look at 'process' in small on-going human interactions, and forswear the attempt at any large-scale cross-sectional validity. The ethnomethodologists (as also the humanistic psychologists) have become impressed by the need for comprehensible models of the way individuals construe reality, models which may be drawn from role-theory or use a play-acting parallel. (Ethnomethodologists form a currently fashionable school of sociologists who, resenting the inevitable bias of 'objective' viewpoints, attempt

118

through participant observation and empathy to avoid such 'objectivication'. For a sympathetic account see Filmer, Phillipson and Silverman, 1972.) The drive is to discover the rules and patterns by which individuals structure their own experience, and the preferred method for discovering these rules and patterns is the microscopic examination of individual interactions. This whole intellectual fashion is in many ways parallel to that which is seen in commercial research. Disappointed by the naiveté and clumsiness of mass-survey methods, researchers retreat into the individual and personal in pursuit of an elusive 'understanding'.

Need for a fresh model

Of course one must sympathize with the point of view. It is true that much survey research in the 'sixties was crude, simplistic and quite probably inaccurate. It is true that careful examination of individual reactions can give more comprehensible pointers towards the way human beings structure their perceptions. Yet it is not good enough for psychologists, sociologists, or theorists of consumer behaviour to retreat into the merely personal and arbitrary where there is no means of judging how generally valid are any results.

This retreat into the personal and arbitrary has perhaps been at its worst in the advertising agencies, who have some power as patrons of commercial research both in their own right and as advisers (apparently disinterested) to major marketing companies. The advertising agencies have rarely welcomed or financed independent research, and of late years have retreated more and more into the use of 'soft data' (usually interpreted reports of group discussion), which has the great advantage of being inconclusive and untestable. The usual method of 'testing' advertisements in London today is to set up two or three group discussions. Consumers are shown early versions of the advertising planned and encouraged to express their comments. This 'research' is intended to discover what impressions the consumers have of the advertising, of what is being communicated. Of course it is a singularly clumsy method of doing the job. Commonly all group discussions are handled and reported on by the same interviewer, whose personal structuring of reality filters all the information. The group method is on the surface of it unsuitable for identifying individual interpretations of messages (even the members of the group themselves will not know whether they personally gained a certain impression from the advertisement, or from fellow group-members' comments on the advertisement). Nor commonly in the report, is any effort made to distinguish the reporter's perceptions of what the consumers perceived in the advertisement, from the reporter's perceptions of what consumer interpretations imply or 'mean', and from the reporter's ideas as to how the advertisement could be adjusted. This muddle is perceived by the users of group discussions as flexibility. The very shapelessness of the results leaves the user free to take what he needs from the results, to perceive them as encouraging or discouraging, as suggesting changes in directions he personally would like, or as providing reasons to toss out entirely advertisements he dislikes. Thus so-called 'research' becomes another tool in a power-game in which the man with the most plausible or persuasive personality can win. And this is not entirely unsatisfactory to the advertising agency. I am not suggesting that agency men favour this kind of procedure for consciously Machiavellian reasons; these are honourable men. I am suggesting that they find these methods comfortable in use, in that they fit the advertising world's customary procedures, based largely on intuition, precedent and personality.

Survey studies and multivariate analysis

This is not to say that multivariate studies and survey studies are non-existent. There has been a growth in the realization that measures of beliefs and attitudes to be really useful should be *continuous*. Services such as the commercially run API (Advertisement Product Index of the British Market Research Bureau) offer simple measurements of agreement or disagreement with certain beliefs about products on a repeat basis, and are widely supported for good reason. Though the measures taken have no very strong theoretic base, the mere fact that the same measures are repeated over similar populations over years makes them useful. Inferences can be drawn from the directions in which the measures move, especially in conjunction with sales trends. The weakness of the API is that though the dimensions used may have been salient when first selected, it cannot monitor the entrance of new beliefs into salience, or their fading from salience.

Multivariate studies attempting to relate demographics, personality measures, beliefs, attitudes, and behaviour also, of course, continue. An interesting development has been the growth of their use in social and community planning areas. Some particularly interesting and technically sophisticated work has been done by the Social Survey Division of the Office of Population Censuses and Surveys, who, among their other tasks, carry out *ad hoc* surveys on a customer contractor basis for government departments. All of their work is worth looking at, but I would particularly mention Bynner (1969) on the causes of adolescent smoking, and Rauter and Hunt (1975) on 'Fifth form girls: their hopes for the future'. These studies have frequently made use of some variant of the trade-off or multidimensional techniques briefly indicated in Chapter 7. Carefully used, these studies can add enormously to planners' perceptions of the needs and values of their public.

The growth of psychographics

There is one other area of current consumer behaviour research (besides 'groups') which advertising agencies can claim to have fostered and encouraged. This is the area of 'psychographics', of 'life-style' measures and of segmentation of markets by 'trends'. The impetus to this work is a double one. It has been influenced by the motivation researchers' view of human behaviour, which traces all decisions back to variables of personality or of inner psychological conditioning. And it has also been influenced by the sociologist's view of choice which sees choice as a resultant of society's conditioning; dependent on one's status and position on the world rather than on perceived qualities of the object chosen.

There are a group of techniques now available – 'life-style', 'psychographics', 'Monitor' – which essentially all try to distinguish buyers of a product from non-buyers on measurements of personality type. Students of consumer behaviour have been used to looking at measured demographic differences between buyers and non-buyers (where by 'demographics' is meant such measures as age, income, place of residence, social class), but have frequently found that demographic measures alone fail to show any difference. Segnit, Broadbent and Burnett (1974) write:

> Many attitudes and interests which might be expected to relate to social grade are in fact currently not associated with grade. Take, for example, sympathy with women's rights and gardening. Most people would feel these are upgrade concerns. Our study shows that such interests are indeed concentrated in distinct minorities – but that these are often not well defined by social grade.

	AB %	C1 %	C2 %	DE %
'I have great sympathy with Women's Lib'	26	25	23	26
'Gardening is my favourite pastime'	32	28	27	30

It was because of numerous findings of this type that the concept of personality differences has been eagerly embraced. Perhaps personality measures or measures of opinion will pinpoint the elusive differences between those who choose one thing rather than another?

As Mostyn puts it in her review of the area (Mostyn, 1976):

> There are basically two ways to approach psychological segmentation: interview a cross-section of consumers using a particular personality test – Cattell's, Edward's etc. – and see if product usage is associated with any of the personality types which emerge, for example with aggressive or authoritarian people. Or, having identified the users of a particular product, submit both users and non-users to a battery of personality tests in order to determine what personality profile best describes users.

The second method has been the most usual. Some investigators (e.g. Evans, 1962) have used personality measures such as the Edward's Personal Preference Schedule developed outside the consumer behaviour area. Eysenck's and Cattell's measure (see E2) have been frequently used. Still more investigators have devised scales and measures of their own. The 'life-style' technique uses measures of individual's opinions and views to achieve segmentation. 'Monitor' a

122

commercial service initiated in America discovers/identifies 'trends' in popular opinion – for example, a growing trend towards mysticism or a decreasing trend towards conformity, and then scores users and non-users of products according to whether they are high on this trend, or low on it.

Many applications of these techniques have been reported in the commercial literature and they have been very widely used and sold. A psychologist, however, cannot but be struck by the poverty of validation for any of the measures used in the published literature. Personality measurement is a notoriously difficult field. As Peck and Whitlow conclude in their volume in this series (D3) all attempts to validate personality theories or measures outside the laboratory 'find inconsistent or at best very weak relationships'. To attempt to separate users from non-users by measures in themselves so weak is difficult. Many studies really turn out to have discriminated users from non-users simply on one single statement of opinion or preference. This single statement . . . it could be something as simple as 'I prefer the traditional way of doing things' . . . is inflated to produce a whole (possibly imaginary) distinction between the personalities of buyers and non-buyers.

The attempt to use personality or life-style measures to illuminate consumer behaviour is an interesting one; but no convincing or coherent theory or testing lies behind it.

Fresh theoretic work

The past few years have been times of financial stringency for marketing and advertising people and there has been little funding available for fresh theoretic work into the nature of consumer behaviour. (Funding for research in this area has almost always had to be privately raised, due to the failure of the Social Science Research Council or the universities and business schools to support work out of the commercial context. I shall return to this point in my final chapter.) Corlett's work of 1974 (p. 52 above) remains the most interesting recent theoretical advance, but is urgently in need of further expansion, perhaps by panel studies examining the relationship of growth in brand-use through frequency of purchase to growth in brand-use due to more people buying.

Some work has emanated from advertising agencies and from private consultants which has attempted to show the relationship of advertising weights (i.e. the amount of money spent on advertising) to movements in sales. None of it has been very convincing, though some of it has been much sold. A published study by MacDonald (1970) has shown (through use of consumer diaries) that there is a fractionally greater likelihood of a consumer switching the brand of a product she purchases, after she has had more opportunities to see advertising. However the problem with all work that attempts to relate the amount of advertising seen *directly* to shift in sales, is that it totally neglects the scientifically well-established fact that some persuasive communications may result in changes in behaviour, some may not. It is perhaps odd that this basic research work patronized by an advertising agency, should be work which neglects the likelihood that some ads work and some don't. At a practitioner level, advertising agencies are convinced that it matters enormously what an advertisement says; they recognize that some forms of communication may not 'change the minds' of the consumer at all, or worse, may change it in a negative direction. At the level of basic research, they patronize work which neglects entirely any variation of effect from advertisement to advertisement.

It seems to me that there is an urgent need for studies which will relate communications to changes in attitudes, norms and intentions; will relate these to changes in behavioural intention and behaviour, and to changes in frequency of purchase and of numbers purchasing. And will do all these things over successive time periods. Fishbein's theories are stressed in this book because they (perhaps alone) offer operational techniques for doing this job.

However such studies have not so far been set up. Market researchers are more interested in providing techniques which they can patent as their own alone; most advertising agencies (perhaps not unnaturally) have tended to spend their research and development money on providing general 'think-piece' essays based on assertion or a few group discussions, which can be used to impress their clients. Cranfield School of Management is one of the few business schools which have attempted to look at consumer behaviour in any detailed way in their ongoing study of advertising research (see, for example, Corkindale and Kennedy, 1974, 1976). But so far this work has gone little further than producing useful surveys of the kinds of technique in use, and some sensible commonsense advice. One must wait to see whether it will break fresh theoretic ground.

It must be accepted that the prime job of commercial advertising agencies and market research companies is to address themselves to short-term tasks. What shall they put in next season's advertisements for such and such a product? This *ad hoc* task may sometimes best be approached through small-scale and intuitive studies. Huge, block-busting, multi-variate researches rarely help the copywriter very much. But if the persuasion industry is ever to command real respect and understanding, it should also address itself to basic theoretic modelling problems. It is with the elucidation of these problems that we have been concerned in this book.

Conclusion and summary

This chapter has attempted to survey, in a brief and neces-sarily somewhat opinionated form, the kind of activity in consumer behaviour studies currently popular. I have argued that the over-use of ill thought out multivariate techniques in the 'sixties, together with the continued popularity of 'motiva-tion research', led to an overwhelming upsurge of group dis-cussion work. Advertising agencies encouraged and promoted this trend to the detriment of any more intellectually reputable procedures. Survey studies of attitudes and beliefs have continued to be used, the only fresh technical developments being in the area of multi-dimensional scaling and trade-off analysis, both of which present problems in interpretation. A great deal of work has gone into the area loosely known as psychographics, without producing any very clear advance. Theoretic work has on the whole been neglected.

9
Applied work with expectancy-value theory

In Chapters 5 and 6, it was suggested that the most interesting new model of choice behaviour emerging from psychology was the expectancy-value model associated particularly with Fishbein's work. In Chapter 6, I gave a brief outline of the nature of this model. In the past decade its usage has been growing steadily in the field of consumer behaviour research. In this chapter I shall give some idea of the kind of research which has been done.

Fishbein's own studies

The earliest studies were carried out by Fishbein and his associates in the USA. Fishbein first stated his formulation of an expectancy-value model as early as 1963 with reference to attitudes towards Negroes. He constructed a set of ten modal salient beliefs for his subject population by taking the ten attributes that were elicited most frequently in response to the question: 'What do you believe to be the characteristics of Negroes?' He then took measures of these salient beliefs from a similar population on both the belief-strength or B dimension (probability scales such as likely–unlikely; probable–improbable were used), and on the evaluative or e dimension (using evaluative scales asking whether the attributes named in the salient beliefs were perceived as good–bad, pleasant–unpleasant, etc.). Each subject's attitude towards 'Negroes' was also assessed directly by asking him to rate the concept

'Negro' on five evaluative semantic differential scales. The sum of the responses over these five scales was used as an estimate of attitude. A correlation of 0·80 was obtained between the $\Sigma B_i e_i$ measure and the independent measure of attitude.

This work was interesting in suggesting support for Fishbein's attitude equation. Other studies offered support for Fishbein's behaviour equation; and there are many studies in the psychological literature in which these equations have been tested (see *Attitudes and Behaviour*, K. Thomas (ed.) for accessible reprints of some of them; for an up-to-date review see Fishbein and Ajzen, 1975). However, though throwing theoretic light on choice behaviour, none of them can be considered as applied studies of choice behaviour itself in the real-world situation.

Political studies

Some of the first applications of the Fishbein model were in the area of political behaviour. In a continuing series of studies, Fishbein and his associates (e.g. Fishbein and Feldman, 1963; Fishbein and Coombs, 1974) investigated the relation between beliefs about political candidates and attitudes towards those candidates. In the month prior to the 1964 presidential election, for example, over 600 residents of a small midwestern community were interviewed. The respondents, who were of voting age, expressed their agreement or disagreement with a set of belief statements concerning each of the two presidential candidates, Johnson and Goldwater. In addition, they evaluated each attribute in the belief statements and provided direct measures of their attitudes towards the two candidates.

The belief statements measured had been elicited as 'salient beliefs' from an independent but matched sample of subjects in the same community. The estimates of attitudes towards Johnson and Goldwater arrived at from the salient beliefs through an application of the $B_i e_i$ equation, correlated 0·69 and 0·87 with direct measures of attitude to Johnson and Goldwater, thus providing strong support for the expectancy-value model. Similar results were found in studies dealing with attitudes towards other presidential candidates as well as candidates for the House of Representatives and the Senate.

The same expectancy-value model was recently used in a two-wave panel study of the October 1974 British general election (Fishbein, Thomas and Jaccard, 1976). The sampling plan was to interview 90 eligible voters in each of four constituencies: one safe Labour and one safe Conservative, one marginal Labour and one marginal Conservative. Within each constituency 30 voters who identified with the Labour party, 30 with the Liberal party and 30 with the Conservative party were contacted on the five days immediately prior to the election. Interviewing was done on a quota basis within each constituency with each interviewer (from Taylor–Nelson Associates) assigned a specific quota. In the week following the election an attempt was made to reinterview all respondents. The sampling requirements were reasonably well met (for full details see original paper).

The study was a complex one and full details of design cannot be given here; but (among other things) the questionnaires were designed so as to measure the voters' perceptions of the stands of each candidate, party and party leader on the relevant issues of the campaign; the voters' own evaluations of the values associated with those issues, and his attitudes towards the candidates, parties and party leaders. This information was sufficient to test Fishbein's attitudinal model. The questionnaires also measured the respondent's attitudes towards 'voting for' each of the three candidates standing in his constituency, his normative beliefs concerning 'voting for' each of the candidates (i.e. his belief that others expected him to vote for that candidate) and his intention to vote for each of the three candidates. Data concerning actual voting behaviour was also obtained. This information was sufficient to test the behaviour part of Fishbein's model.

The study provided a mass of fascinating detail about the differing beliefs and attitudes of Conservative, Liberal and Labour voters. Its general thrust was to show (to quote the authors) 'that the British voter, like his American counterpart, is a relatively well-informed, intelligent decision maker who is aware of differences between candidates, parties and party leaders'. In addition the study showed (through measures which have not been described) that the British voter is well aware of the strategic implications of his vote and how much it is likely to affect outcomes at either constituency or national level; and that this knowledge affects his voting intentions and behaviour. This information is of particular interest to politicians.

On the technical 'modelling' side, which must interest those of us searching for generalizable models of choice behaviour, the study offered good support for expectancy-value theory. The correlations between $\Sigma B_i e_i$ and attitude (A_0) were as shown in the table below:

Table 9.1 Correlations between overall attitude towards the candidates, parties and party leaders (A_0) and estimates of these attitudes based on beliefs about their stands on the issues ($\Sigma B_i e_i$)

		Labour	Conservative
A_0	$\Sigma B_i e_i$ (candidate)	0·653	0·576
A_0	$\Sigma B_i e_i$ (party leader)	0·679	0·618
A_0	$\Sigma B_i e_i$ (party)	0·737	0·668

These correlations are all high and significant though, as the authors point out, somewhat lower than those found by Fishbein and Coombs (1974). The study had not allowed for a variation of salient beliefs among constituencies and voters with different party attachments, and this could be expected to depress correlations. However the results undoubtedly support the notion that a voter's attitude to political parties, candidates and leaders are a function of his beliefs.

The study's results also provided support for the notion that a voter's behaviour is a function of his behavioural intention, which in turn is a function of his attitude towards 'voting for that candidate' and his subjective norm concerning 'voting for that candidate'. The following results are presented:

	Single correlations with behaviour Aact and SN		Multiple correlation with behaviour Aact and SN
Labour	0·847	0·633	0·852
Conservative	0·814	0·690	0·838

It is possible to tell by looking at the weights of the regression equation which arrives at the multiple correlation (see pp. 79–80) which component of the equation contributes most towards the final prediction of behaviour. The weights showed that the contribution of the normative side of the equation was low, though slightly higher for the Conservative (0.267) than for Labour (0.121). The inference is that voting behaviours at the 1974 election was more dependent on attitude and its underlying beliefs than on perceptions of how one is expected to vote (the normative component). Further studies on this area would be of great interest to practising politicians, and of considerable relevance to the controversy as to how much voters choose in a rational way and how much their choices are dependent on tribal loyalties and normative perceptions.

The study under discussion was small and cheap. But as far as it goes it suggests the British voter (at least in 1974) applied an open mind knowledgeable as to the stands of parties' candidates and party leaders, to his decision as to his voting behaviour.

Applications in commercial research

Since about 1970 expectancy-value models have been used occasionally in the world of commercial research and some of this work has been published (for British experience, see for instance Tuck and Nelson, 1969; Tuck 1971, 1973; and Cowling, 1972).

In a recent review of consumer psychology in the mid-seventies published in the journal of the European Society of Market Research, Veldhoven of Tilburg University comments that the study of consumer decision making and in particular of expectancy-value models have played a major part in mid-seventies developments (Veldhoven, 1976). Yet it is my belief that expectancy-value models have been more talked about than actually used in the commercial area. They appeared on the scene at about the same time as the backlash against the kind of study described at p. 42 above and when small-scale intuitive studies were growing in popularity. Somehow Fishbein's models became associated with purely mathematical techniques such as those fading in popularity. There is evidence in published work that expectancy-value models are

130

flexible and economic in use and can illuminate marketing decisions. But this has by and large not got through to the world of commercial researchers and the models have not been used at all widely.

They have been used more frequently in non-commercial areas. Interesting recent studies include an examination of women's motivations in choosing different methods of birth control (Jaccard and Davidson, 1972), and a recent study of choices of mode of transport (Thomas, 1976). The transport study is perhaps of particular interest in that it has been published in very full and careful detail and the fieldwork was thoroughly supervised. The study investigated women's behaviour, norms, attitudes and beliefs concerning the acts 'using the bus next week to do my main shopping in Brentford', 'using the car next week to do my main shopping in Brentford' and 'walking next week to do my main shopping in Brentford'. The relationships postulated by the expectancy-value model were consistently found with correlations between the predicted elements of the model at high 0·7 and 0·8 levels. The study was able to lay out precisely the beliefs and norms which influenced housewives in their choice of transport mode, and to monitor changes in strength and salience of belief subsequent to a fare increase.

Conclusion and summary

Sufficient applied studies exist to show the utility and validity of the expectancy-value model of Fishbein in the study of such differing areas of consumer behaviour as political behaviour, choice of mode of transport, choice of birth control method, choice of job. The model has been much talked about in the world of commercial research but actual applications have as yet been few and far between. The model has suffered from association with other multivariate models for consumer behaviour studies which have been found cumbrous and misleading. Perhaps its time is yet to come.

10
End-piece

So where have we got to? We have surveyed a great many theories of consumer behaviour, both explicit and implicit, we have looked at some of the insights into consumer behaviour offered by the psychologists, and we have indicated some of the research which is currently going on.

The final picture is a fluid one. There are no certainties. Worse than this, there are no settled methods of procedure and no on-going centre of studies. Anyone who has followed this book so far will realize that there are promising ideas and theories in the consumer behaviour area; but, in Europe especially, this is a field which has suffered through the lack of any centre of research and development.

Oddly enough, though the United Kingdom market research industry spends a great deal of money every year on *ad hoc* and continuous measurement studies (estimated 1975 expenditure = £44 million), there is a great shortage of finance for any real development work. The British market research industry is split up into many small firms, all operating on very narrow profit margins. In 1976 about 60 per cent of all market research agencies listed in the Market Research Society Yearbook employed less than ten executive and office staff. A highly competitive and fragmented industry of this kind cannot generate funds for basic research or for comparison of techniques.

The Market Research Society of Great Britain does excellent work in organizing educational programmes, in professional seminars and in publishing journals. But a society with only 700 or so full members, most of them full-time practitioners in a competitive business, simply cannot generate the quality of development work necessary on a voluntary basis. As it is, the amount of work done by the Market Research Society, entirely self-financed, is extraordinary. There can be few other professional societies so active. But they cannot alone do enough.

Nor have the advertisers or advertising agencies filled the gap. They have been willing enough to organize the excellent media studies which monitor the readership and viewership of various advertising media. But they have never, even in the prosperous days of the 'sixties, seen it as their business to join together to finance real development work in the understanding of consumer behaviour, or even of the narrower topic 'how advertising works'. One cannot help suspecting that they would not welcome scientific testing of their procedures, based largely as they are on hunch, precedent and intuition. But I do not think the explanation is so simple. Advertising is an in-bred and defensive industry, and quite genuinely (and often with reason) tends to classify 'outsiders' as both ignorant and hostile. Too many economists and sociologists have criticized the industry with complete lack of understanding. Is it to be wondered at that advertising men do not exactly welcome the attention of social scientists?

One might have expected the business schools or university departments of psychology and sociology to fill the gap. For varying reasons they have not done so. Cranfield School of Management has done some small-scale work financed by a consortium of advertisers. London Business School has given Professor Ehrenberg a platform. But no business school has produced a vital Department of Consumer Behaviour which is a centre of on-going research. Their emphasis has been much more in the economic, accounting and financial areas. University departments of social psychology and sociology have rarely taken consumer behaviour or market-place choice behaviour as a topic for study; perhaps because the dominant intellectual climate among behavioural scientists has been hostile to capitalism and to economic liberalism. Another factor holding back university attention to this area has been that English academic snobbishness which tends to feel that Ph.D.s can have little to learn from the techniques and theories of applied researchers, even though these may carry out more research in one year than the average academic gets through in a lifetime.

A hope for the future

Yet enough has been said in this book to show that there *are* promising lines for consumer behaviour research available. The British market research profession is one of high expertise and efficiency. Anyone who has attended the annual conferences of ESOMAR (the European Society of Market Research) will know that their technical expertise is perhaps the most highly regarded in the world. Their contribution to export business is constantly growing and British researchers are on the way to becoming the world's specialists in research in the under-developed countries. All this expertise needs only a little encouragement to achieve a real breakthrough in understanding and in achievement. Nor would the results be only of use in the marketing and commercial area (though, heaven knows, this is an important enough area for a trading nation). Any democratic society which relies on 'planners' needs to be expert in understanding the beliefs, desires and choices of its people. All social research is desperately in need of adequate and operational models of human choice.

The Social Science Research Council's Survey Research Unit, under the direction of Mark Abrahams, went some way, on a small budget, to achieving the kind of work I have in mind. But the Survey Research Unit is to be closed down. What is needed is some research department attached to a major university which would act as a centre both for studies in consumer behaviour and for the dissemination of research techniques. Such a research department would ideally be funded partly through the SSRC and partly through donations from industry and consortia of advertisers. If it could run a one year M.Sc. in consumer behaviour theory and survey research techniques, this could be of inestimable value to all those many geographers, sociologists, social psychologists, economists, architects and others who emerge from their undergraduate studies each year, anxious to engage in research about the views and choices of the people, but ignorant of basic survey research techniques, ignorant of the body of work which already exists in examining consumer mental processes and decisions which this book has described.

Objections

It could be objected that too much of the work that exists is on too intellectually low a level to interest university researchers. But much can be learned from false starts. And part of the reason that consumer behaviour theory and research has not advanced as quickly as it might have done, is the absence of any truly high-calibre research centre.

It might be thought that we in this country can safely leave advances in this field to the USA or to the other Europeans. Institutes of consumer behaviour studies exist all over Europe and North America. But I believe that this area is too important for us to leave technical advance to others, and also believe that there is a specifically British contribution to be made.

Conclusion

It may seem an odd conclusion to a book of this kind, aimed mainly at surveying a field for students, to end with a fervent plea for finance and a place for further research into that field. But consumer behaviour studies are something of a Cinderella. Students of the field will know that they have little formal place in the British academic system. I believe these studies have made a useful beginning – a beginning I have tried to survey in this book. But the major need now is for further research which should be carried out in conjunction with methodological studies and the critical and thorough teaching of survey research techniques. Such research requires a centre and finance where it can be carried out. Perhaps one day these things will come.

References and
Name Index

*The numbers in italics following entries refer to page numbers
within this book.*

Aaker, D. A. and Morgan, S. M. (1971) Modelling store choice
behaviour. *Journal of Marketing Research 8*: 38–42. *34*

Barnes, M. (ed.) (1975) *The Three Faces of Advertising*. London:
The Advertising Association.

Blumler, J. G. and McQuail, D. (1968) *Television in Politics:
Its Uses and Influence*. London: Faber & Faber (also Chicago
University Press, 1969). *88*

Bruce, John (1972) First experiences with Fishbein theory and
survey methods: a case study. *Proceedings of the ESOMAR
Madrid Seminar on Advanced Advertising Theories and Research*. Amsterdam: European Society of Market Research
(ESOMAR).

Butler, D. and Stokes D. (1969) *Political Change in Britain:
Forces Shaping Electoral Choice*. London: Macmillan. *56*

Bynner, J. M. (1969) *The Young Smoker*. London: HMSO.
121

Campbell, D. T. (1957) Factors relevant to the validity of
experiments in social settings. *Psychological Bulletin 54*:
297–312.

Campbell, A., Converse, P. E., Miller, W. E. and Stokes, D. E.
(1960) *The American Voter*. New York: Wiley. *55*

Christopher, M. (1973) Non-metric scaling: the principles and
marketing possibilities. *European Research 1*, 3: 108–14. *105*

Corkindale, D. K. and Kennedy, S. H. (1974) *Managing Advertising Effectively*. Bradford: MCB Books. *124*

Corkindale, D. K. and Kennedy, S. H. (1976) *Managing the Advertising Process*. Farnborough, Hants: Saxon House/Cranfield Institute Press. *124*

Corlett, T. (1974) Consumer purchasing patterns: a different perspective. ADMAP (June). *52–3, 123*

Cowling, A. B. (1972) Consequences of applying the Fishbein model to advertising planning. *Proceedings of the ESOMAR Madrid Seminar on Advanced Advertising Theories and Research*. Amsterdam: European Society of Market Research (ESOMAR). *130*

Crewe, I. (1974) Do Butler and Stokes really explain political change in Britain? *European Journal of Political Research 2*: 47–92. *56*

Dixon, T. H. and Horton, D. E. (eds) (1968) *Verbal Behavior and S-R Behavior Theory*. Englewood Cliffs, N.J.: Prentice-Hall. *77*

Dulany, D. E. (1968) Awareness, rules and propositional control: a confrontation with S-R behavior theory. In T. H. Dixon and D. E. Horton (eds) *Verbal Behavior and S-R Behavior Theory*. Englewood Cliffs, N.J.: Prentice-Hall. *76–7*

Edwards, A. L. and Kenney, K. C. (1946) A comparison of the Thurstone and Likert technique of attitude scale construction. *Journal of Applied Psychology 30*: 72–83. *69*

Edwards, W. (1954) The theory of decision making. *Psychological Bulletin 51*: 380–418. *71–2*

Ehrenberg, A. S. C. (1972) *Repeat-buying, Theory and Applications*. Amsterdam and New York: North Holland Publishing Company. *31, 33, 34–36*

Engel, J. F., Kollat, D. T. and Blackwell, R. D. (1968) *Consumer Behavior*, New York: Holt Rinehart and Winston. *19, 26–7*

Evans, F. B. (1962) Correlates of automobile shopping behavior. *Journal of Marketing Research 26*: 74–7. *122*

Fallan, E. and Tuck, M. (1973) How simple elicitation helped solve an advertising problem: a case history. *From Market Research to Advertising Strategy and Vice Versa, Proceedings of the ESOMAR Lisbon Seminar Nov/Dec 1973*. Amsterdam: European Society of Market Research (ESOMAR). *96*

Farley, J. V. and Ring, L. W. (1970) An empirical test of the

Howard-Sheth model of buyer behavior. *Journal of Marketing Research* 7: 427–38. *31*

Filmer, P., Phillipson, M., Silverman, D. and Walsh, D. (1972) *New Directions in Sociological Theory*. London: Collier-Macmillan. *119*

Fishbein, M. (ed.) (1967) *Readings in Attitude Theory and Measurement*. New York: Wiley. *64, 73, 74ff*

Fishbein, M. and Ajzen, I. (1972) Attitudes and opinions. *Annual Review of Psychology* 23: 487–544. *63*

Fishbein, M. and Ajzen, I. (1975) *Belief, Attitude, Intention and Behavior: An Introduction to Theory and Research*. Reading, Mass.: Addison-Wesley. *73, 92, 127*

Fishbein, M. and Coombes, F. S. (1974) Basis for decision: an attitudinal analysis of voting behaviour. *Journal of Applied Social Psychology* 4: 95–124. *56, 127*

Fishbein, M. and Feldman, S. (1963) Social psychological studies in voting behavior 1: Theoretical and methodological considerations. *Journal of Applied Social Psychology* 4: 95–124. *127*

Fishbein, M., Thomas, K. and Jaccard, J. J. (1976) *A Study of the October 1974 General Election in UK*. SSRC Survey Research Unit paper. *56, 128*

Goodhardt, G. J., Ehrenberg, A. S. C. and Collins, M. A. (1975) *The Television Audience: Patterns of Viewing*. Farnborough, Hants: Saxon House. *36*

Howard, J. A. and Sheth, J. N. (1969) *The Theory of Buyer Behavior*. New York: Wiley. *21, 27–33*

Jaccard, J. J. and Davidson, A. R. (1972) Towards an understanding of family planning behaviors: an initial investigation. *Journal of Applied Social Psychology* 2: 228–35. *131*

Kaplan, K. J. and Fishbein, M. (1969) The source of beliefs, their saliency and prediction of attitude. *Journal of Social Psychology* 78: 63–74. *88*

Katona, G. (1960) *The Powerful Consumer*, New York: McGraw-Hill. *48*

Keenan, Kate M. (1976) *Reasons for Joining and Early Termination of Service in WRAC*. Report no. 24/75, Ministry of Defence Personnel Research Establishment, Farnborough, Hants. *93–100*

Klapper, J. (1960) *The Effects of Mass Communication*. Glencoe, California: Free Press. *55*

Lazarsfeld, P. F., Berelson, B. R. and Gaudet, H. (1948) *The*

People's Choice: How the Voter Makes Up his Mind in a Presidential Campaign. New York: Columbia University Press (revised edition 1968). *55*

Lipstein, B. (1959) The dynamics of brand loyalty and brand switching. *Proceedings of the 1959 A.R.F. Conference.* New York: Advertising Research Foundation. *33*

MacDonald, C. (1970) What is the short-term effect of advertising? *ESOMAR 1970 Congress Proceedings.* Also printed in ADMAP November 1970, 350–6 and 366. *124*

Medawar, P. (1967) *The Art of the Soluble: Creativity and Originality in Science,* London: Methuen. *29*

Miller, G. A. (1956) The Magic Number Seven plus or minus two: some limits on our capacity for processing information. *Psychological Review 63:* 81–97. *88*

Moser, C. A. and Kalton, G. (1971) *Survey Methods in Social Investigation.* London: Heinemann (revised edition; original publication 1958). *75*

Mostyn, Barbara (1976) *Motivational Research – Passing Phase or Permanent Feature?* Occasional Paper, Cranfield School of Management, Marketing Communications Research Centre. *116, 122*

Nicosia, F. M. (1966) *Consumer Decision Processes.* Englewood Cliffs, New Jersey: Prentice-Hall. *20–6*

Nicosia, F. M. (1968) Advertising management, consumer behavior and simulation. *Journal of Advertising Research 8:* 29–37.

Ogilvy, D. (1963) *Confessions of an Advertising Man.* London: Longman.

Oppenheim, A. N. (1966) *Questionnaire Design and Attitude Measurement.* London: Heinemann Educational. *64, 75*

Osgood, C. E., Suci, G. J. and Tannenbaum, P. H. (1957) *The Measurement of Meaning.* Urbana: University of Illinois Press. *69, 102*

Peck, D. and Whitlow, D. (1975) *Approaches to Personality Theory.* London: Methuen (*Essential Psychology D3*). *123*

Packard, Vance (1957) *The Hidden Persuaders.* London: Longman (Penguin edition, 1960). *41*

Popper, K. (1972) *Objective Knowledge: An Evolutionary Approach.* Oxford University Press. *29*

Rauter, Irene and Hunt, Audrey (1975) *Fifth-form Girls: Their Hopes for the Future.* London: HMSO.

Reich, B. and Adcock, C. (1976) *Values, Attitudes and Behaviour*

Change. London: Methuen (*Essential Psychology B3*). *64, 72–3*

Robinson, J. P. and Shaver, P. R. (1969) *Measures of Social Psychological Attitudes*. Ann Arbor, Mich.: Institute for Social Research. *69*

Rosenberg, M. J. (1956) Cognitive structure and attitudinal affect. *Journal of Abnormal and Social Psychology 53*: 367–72. *73, 102*

Reeves, Rosser (1961) *Reality in Advertising*. London: Mac-Gibbon. *39*

Ryan, T. A. (1970) *Intentional Behavior: An Approach to Human Motivation*. New York: Ronald. *75*

Segnit, S., Broadbent, S. and Burnett, L. (1974) Clustering by product usage: a case history. *The Challenges Facing Market Research: How Do We Meet Them? Proceedings of the ESOMAR Hamburg Congress September 1974*. Amsterdam: European Society of Market Research. *122*

Shaw, M. F. and Wright, J. M. (1967) *Scales for the Measurement of Attitudes*. New York: McGraw-Hill. *69*

Sheth, J. N. and Park, C. W. (1973) *Equivalence of Fishbein and Rosenberg Theories of Attitudes*. Faculty Working Paper No. 108, College of Commerce and Business Administration, University of Illinois. *102*

Thomas, Kerry (ed.) (1971) *Attitudes and Behaviour*. Harmondsworth: Penguin. *65, 127*

Thomas, Kerry (1975) The use of a modified expectancy-value model in the forecasting of off-peak travel behaviour. Centre for Transport Studies, Cranfield Institute of Technology, Cranfield Institute of Technology.

Thomas, Kerry (1976) A reinterpretation of the attitude approach to transport mode choice and an exploratory empirical test. *Environment and Planning* (in press). *129*

Thomas, K. and Tuck, M. (1975) An exploratory study of determinant and indicant beliefs in attitude measurement. *European Journal of Social Psychology 5*: 167–87. *88*

Tolman, E. C. (1932) *Purposive Behavior in Animals and Men*. New York: Appleton-Century-Crofts. *102*

Treasure, John (1975) How advertising works. In Michael Barnes (ed.) *The Three Faces of Advertising*. London: The Advertising Association. *48, 52*

Tuck, M. (1971) Practical frameworks for advertising planning and research. *Proceedings of the Madrid Seminar on Advanced*

Advertising Theories and Research, European Society of Market Research.

Tuck, M. (1971) Purchasing and persuasion. ADMAP (June). *130*

Tuck, M. (1973) Fishbein theory and the Bass-Talarzyk problem. *Journal of Marketing Research 10*: 345–8. *130*

Tuck, M. and Nelson, E. (1969) The relationship between attitudes and behaviour. *ESOMAR Congress Papers 1969*. Amsterdam: European Society of Market Research. *130*

Tuncalp, S. and Sheth, J. N. (1974) Predictions of attitudes: a comparative study of the Rosenberg, Fishbein and Sheth models. *Proceedings of the Association for Consumer Research*. *102*

Twyman, W. A. (1973) Designing advertiser research for marketing decisions. *Journal of the Market Research Society 15*, 2: 77–100. *118*

Veblen, Thorsten (1899) *The Theory of the Leisure Class*. London: Macmillan. *47*

Veldhoven, G. M. van (1976) Consumer psychology in the mid-seventies: developments and trends. *European Research 4*, 2: 84–96. *130*

Westwood, D., Lunn, T. and Beazley, D. (1974) The trade-off model and its extension. *Journal of the Market Research Society* (July). *108*

Wicker, A. W. (1969) An examination of the 'other variables' explanation of attitude-behavior inconsistency. *Journal of Personality and Social Psychology 19*: 18–30. *65*

Subject Index

143